OUR CHANGING EARTH

Why Climate Change Matters to Young People

Arjun Marwaha

*Especially dedicated to the young
who will inherit the earth.*

*Thank you very much to Alex Hall,
whose expertise in the field offered perspective,
and Greg Kaplan for guidance and assistance.*

TABLE OF CONTENTS

PREFACE

We have all heard of global warming and its effect on global climate (i.e., climate change). But what do they mean? How are they related with each other? What do they mean for the Earth and how will future generations be affected?

This book seeks to not only investigate the historical, scientific causes of global warming, but also its earthly and health-related effects. Ramifications range from impact on biological systems, such as the rise of vector-borne diseases, to environmental consequences, such as the rise of oceanic levels. In an effort to promote a message to the younger generations, this book seeks to leave readers with a thought-provoking idea: the future of our Earth is in our hands and we must decide how to preserve our home.

I am a 16 year-old human-being. I know the Earth that future generations will walk upon one day. I have studied history and how this "industrialization" is not only linked but is now also scientifically proven to be connected to the deterioration of our Earth. I have seen first-hand the extreme effects on precipitation and heard saddening stories about the melting ice caps. I, and I am confident others, can see the existence of the phenomenon and its threat to society. This book encourages all humans — of any age, social status, and ethnicity — to raise awareness about global warming and, most importantly, to take heed of its various impacts on future generations.

PART I

PRESENT SCENARIO

History and Past, Greenhouse
Gases, Politicization

CHAPTER 1

HISTORY AND PAST

Earth, before humans stepped on it:

The natural world was at an equilibrium. Lava and other chemicals spewed from volcanoes during an eruption. This particulate matter incited climatic changes, some of which prompted periodic phases of global warming. This magnificent natural phenomenon was counteracted by the Ice Ages, comprised of intermittent glacial periods chilling the Earth and all of its inhabitants. Variations in Earth's orbit, fluctuations in ocean current, and the deviations in solar energy/intensity from the sun were among the plausible explanations for major climatic shifts and trends. However, these forces balanced one another, allowing us to conceptualize Earth's 4.6 billion-year-old climate as a **sinusoidal** wave — peaks and troughs frequent the graph, but this continuum serves to maintain the equilibrium of Earth's air temperatures. More importantly, the data supports that there is no singular trend of global warming (or cooling, for that matter); everything is split into phases, not an unchangeable ultimatum such as we face today. Generally speaking, climate changes prior to noticeable human activity (roughly the 1700s) can be explained by natural causes, including changes in solar energy, volcanic eruptions, and natural changes in greenhouse gas (greenhouse gas) concentrations.

Volcanoes play a key role in the regulation of Earth's climate and air temperatures. Following an eruption, gases and dust particles would be discharged into the air, thereby blocking the incoming solar radiation. These hovering gases include the abundant, but harmless, water vapor, sulfur dioxide, and hydrogen sulfide. Sulfur dioxide can react with water vapor in the air to produce the sulfuric acid aerosols — a haze of tiny droplets — that shield the atmosphere from energy from the sun, causing cooling of the local region. The droplets can last for up to three years in the stratosphere and when moved around by the wind they can cause significant cooling worldwide.

Conversely, volcanic carbon dioxide, a greenhouse gas, has the potential to promote global warming. Though global concentrations of these gases do not change much, historical periods of intense volcanism have significantly increased the emissions of greenhouse gases. Therefore, the increase in carbon dioxide concentration drives global warming.

In the pre-industrial era, natural causes like volcanic eruptions did affect the global climate due to carbon dioxide emissions and volcanic aerosols, but these are now dwarfed by human emissions. The U.S. Geographical Survey reports that human activities now emit more than 135 times as much CO2 as volcanoes each year.[2] The natural phenomenon of eruptions historically has had a powerful impact on the climate, whether it was a cooling or warming of the air temperatures.

In addition to volcanism, changes in the sun's intensity have influenced Earth's climate in the past. For example, the so-called "Little Ice Age" between the 17th and 19th centuries may have been caused by a low solar activity phase from 1645 to 1715, which coincided with cooler temperatures.[1] This was known in climate science as the Maunder Minimum, in which sunspots became exceedingly rare. Sunspots come in pairs of opposite magnetic polarity, and are typically indicative of an increase of powerful radiation. As the weather became abnormally frigid, sunspot occurrence was at a minimum leading towards the positive correlation of solar activity and sunspots. Events like the one described above, and countless others, are easily explained through the natural fluctuations in the sun's intensity; temperature is simply a physical quantity measuring thermodynamics, or the relationships between heat energy and all other energy. Thus, alterations in the Sun's intensity (our source of heat) will dramatically impact the surface temperatures of Earth, as is evident historically.

Moreover, these changes in solar energy continue to affect climate. Known as the solar cycle, this roughly 11-year periodic process has fluctuations in sunspot quantity and levels of solar radiation. At the time of this writing, Solar Cycle 24, a time with low levels of solar radiation and fewer sunspots, is drawing to a close. Unfortunately, in this most recent solar cycle, solar output has been lower than it has been since the mid-20th century and therefore cannot explain the recent warming of the earth.[1] Similar to volcanic eruptions, human activity has significantly outpaced the effects of solar activity in the past decades. Nevertheless, it is important to recognize the key natural phenomena that have induced climatic trends historically; these natural phenomena allow for a comparison to the severe repercussions of human activity on global warming.

Scientific research supports that, modern climate changes cannot be explained by natural causes alone. Research mandated by the federal government indicates that natural causes do not explain most observed warming especially warming since the mid-20th century. Rather, it is extremely likely that human activities have been the dominant cause of that warming.[1] Through a simple scientific understanding of the greenhouse effect (covered later in Part I) and a glance at the measured observations and dire trends, global warming has been proven as a real phenomenon, discrediting those who remain skeptical of the climatic event. Moreover, human activities have overwhelmingly contributed to a rise in greenhouse gas concentrations, prompting the warming of Earth at a global scale.1 Before addressing the current scenario, let us inspect how humans introduced industrialization and hence, unwittingly, greenhouse gases into the atmosphere.

The Industrial Revolution, beginning in the 1760s, signaled the first changes in the atmosphere due to human activity. The changes arose from the increased burning of **fossil fuels** (oil and gas) to meet the energy needs of factories, power plants and new modes of transport. This burning of fossil fuels released huge amounts of carbon dioxide and other **greenhouse gases** (greenhouse gas) into the atmosphere. These potent gases would progressively lead to global warming, which has increased exponentially to the present day. The specifics of the present scenario of global warming will be explained in the following chapter.

Although the Industrial Revolution, as a historical era, 'ended' in the 1840s, industrialization itself has continued at an ever-increasing rate: atmospheric CO_2 concentrations have grown 40% since pre-industrial times, from approximately 280 parts per million by volume (ppmv) in the 18th century to over 410 ppmv in mid-2018.[1] The current CO_2 level is higher than it has been in at least 800,000 years, and possibly even the past 20 million years.[1] We are now on track to reach 560 parts per million (double pre-industrial average) in 50 years' time, and 840 ppm (triple pre-industrial average) by the middle of the next century — numbers that begin to approach the daunting records of millions of years ago.

The finding that while liquid water was prevalent, the solar intensity was at extremely low levels made scientists wonder what was causing the extra heat in the atmosphere and lead to a theory that was introduced in 1972. At the time many concepts were considered, but eventually scientists formulated the greenhouse hypothesis in an effort to understand how Earth's atmosphere was able to regulate surface temperatures. This theory largely explains the high historic levels of atmospheric CO_2. In addition to the aforementioned, industrialization has led to a runaway scenario in which human activities currently inject over 30 billion tons of CO_2 into the atmosphere every year.[1] Putting this into perspective, both undersea and land volcanoes generate about 200 million tons of CO_2 annually; the sheer difference between these two numbers prompt fear amongst scientists who have begun to calculate the degree of global warming in the future. These findings by the Intergovernmental Panel on Climate Change have shocked scientists and, frankly, the world.[1] This information is of particular concern for Generation Z who are growing up in the face of these stark realities and will be dealing with them for their futures and their family's futures.

Hopefully, this chapter has not only summed up climate changes and global warming throughout the prehistoric era, but also has highlighted the Industrial Revolution's creation of a turning point in human history: its changes to daily life and drastic effects have led to ever-increasing carbon dioxide emissions that threaten to exacerbate global warming in the future.

CHAPTER 2

GREENHOUSE GASES

Alas, the unprecedented levels of human greenhouse gas emissions have culminated in the bizarre phenomenon of global warming — or is it really that strange? From the generalized skeptic's perspective, global warming is dismissed as a hoax for several reasons but the primary one is a generic distrust in science. More specifically, they don't believe the empirical evidence. In light of this, this chapter will thoroughly explore the scientific processes behind "global warming," and further investigate the scope and specifics of the phenomenon throughout the world.

The term "global warming" was first coined in 1975 in a *Science* article by geochemist Wallace Broecker of Columbia University. The article titled *Climatic Change: Are We on the Brink of a Pronounced Global Warming?* attempted to finally end a major debate at the time. Several scientists during the 1970s recognized the oncoming of a "inadvertent climate modification," but no unanimous decision could be reached to predict the direction of that change (i.e., warming or cooling). More specifically, scientists speculated over the net changes to the atmosphere: for years the industry thought of aerosols, which include haze, smoke, and particulate air pollutants, to be coolants while greenhouse gas emissions were thought to cause warming. In certain amounts, these two could cancel one another out. Ultimately, Broecker's publication correctly predicted the net warming of the earth. In the groundbreaking article described above, the Columbia scholar defined the process as the, "observed century-scale rise in the average temperature of the Earth's climate system."[1] Only later did scientists link this process to the greenhouse effect, which will be explained throughout the rest of the chapter.

Distinguishing between global warming and climate change is essential for upcoming generations. **Global warming** is the result of obtaining more solar radiation due to the greenhouse effect (i.e. increased surface temperatures) while **climate change** is the long-term gradual changes in climate patterns due to global warming itself. Put simply, climate change is the *result* of global warming.

Before understanding the greenhouse effect, we must first understand the equilibrium of **solar radiation** that has kept the Earth at its average surface temperatures for the past 4.6 billion years. The Sun is always shining and directing solar radiation towards the Earth's atmosphere. This radiation is composed of visible light, UV (ultraviolet) radiation, and IR (infrared radiation). The energy of level of UV radiation is higher than that of infrared, and therefore UV radiation has a shorter wavelength than infrared radiation. In general, about 30% of this solar radiation going towards the Earth is immediately reflected back out towards space by clouds, ice, snow, sand, and other surfaces. This leaves about 70% of the radiation is absorbed by the oceans, the land and the atmosphere. As they heat up, the oceans, land and atmosphere release heat in the form of IR thermal radiation, which passes out of the atmosphere and into space. This equilibrium of incoming and outgoing radiation maintains an average surface temperature of 59ºF, making Earth habitable.[3]

Now for the question everyone has been waiting for: what is the greenhouse effect? The **greenhouse effect** causes warming of the Earth's atmosphere, which absorbs solar energy and slows the rate at which the energy escapes to space; it acts like a blanket, insulating and warming the Earth. A simple analogy is a car sitting outside on a cold, sunny day. The incoming solar radiation warms the interior of the car, but outgoing radiation is trapped inside the car's closed windows. The process is explained in the diagram below.

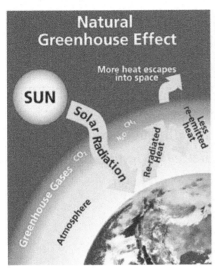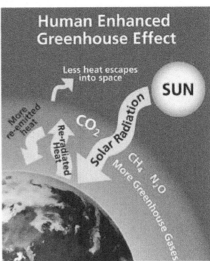

This diagram explains how the greenhouse effect can be enhanced by human activity. Credit to LiveScience.[3]

This process traps the heat in Earth's lower atmosphere, thereby increasing the surface temperatures. The trapping of energy from the sun in Earth's atmosphere and system, and the observable rise in temperature, is known as global warming. As explained by Michael Daley, an associate professor of Environmental Science at Lasell College, "gas molecules that absorb thermal infrared radiation, and are in significant enough quantity, can force the climate system; these are known as greenhouse gases."[3] Therefore, following this line of observation, if the quantified concentration of greenhouse gases is higher, then the greenhouse effect would be accelerated and therefore the rate of global warming would increase.

In understanding this phenomenon and its direct effect (global warming), the types of greenhouse gases in the atmosphere are extremely important factors to consider since some gases may be able to induce warming faster than others. Below some of the most prevalent and potent greenhouse gases found in our atmosphere are explained.

First, in order to understand the ability of a certain gas to cause warming, the term **global warming potential** (GWP) must be defined. This is a measure of how much energy (heat) the emissions of 1 ton of any gas will absorb over a given period of time, relative to the emissions of 1 ton of carbon dioxide (CO_2).[7] Carbon dioxide is set as the standard; thus, the large majority of other greenhouse gases will be much more potent in regards to inducing warming.

Water Vapor (H_2O)

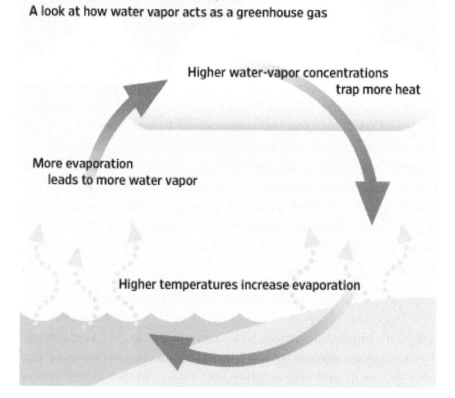

The Cycle of Water Vapor
A look at how water vapor acts as a greenhouse gas

Higher water-vapor concentrations trap more heat

More evaporation leads to more water vapor

Higher temperatures increase evaporation

This diagram explains how water vapor can function as a greenhouse gas. Courtesy of Gautam Naik.[5]

Being the most abundant gas in the atmosphere, water vapor is considered to be a climate feedback rather than a direct result of industrialization. The process is explained and depicted below:

- A warmer atmosphere causes the evaporation of water from oceans, rivers, reservoirs, and soil

- There exists a higher absolute humidity (air is able to 'hold' more water vapor molecules)

- Higher concentration of water vapor in air is then able to absorb more thermal IR energy radiated from Earth

- More absorbed energy further warms the atmosphere

The above process is known as a **positive feedback loop**. Although scientists have a poor understanding of the methods to measure water vapor and its historic levels, scientists can affirm that this repetitive process only exacerbates global warming due to the concepts of the water cycle and **absolute humidity**.[4] Specifically, it has a GWP of 2: pound for pound, the impact of water vapor on warming is double that of carbon dioxide.[4] Thus, despite the fact that water vapor emissions are not caused directly through human activity, it has the capability of wreaking havoc on the current climate system via the greenhouse effect.

Carbon Dioxide (CO_2)

Carbon dioxide is widely regarded as the most prevalent greenhouse gas caused by human activity. This gas occurs naturally in carbon cycle in the following ways:

1. Plant and Animal Respiration

2. Volcanoes (as mentioned earlier)

3. Ocean-atmosphere Exchange.

A certain amount of CO_2 is naturally removed from the atmosphere when absorbed by plants and oceans as part of the biological carbon cycle. Known as **land and ocean sinks**, these geographical features absorb carbon dioxide from the atmosphere and store it. By the numbers, a study published in *Biogeosciences* found that around 56% of the CO_2 is absorbed by land and ocean sinks. This leaves approximately 44% of total human-caused carbon dioxide emissions in the atmosphere.[6] It is the proliferation of the concentration of atmospheric CO_2 that leads to warming thereby accelerating the feedback loop of water vapor. This causes the CO_2 — once absorbed from ocean sinks — to be released back into the atmosphere, due to the higher concentration of water and absolute humidity as previously explained. In addition, CO_2 remains in the atmosphere for thousands of years.[7]

Breaking down the sectors of CO_2, the gas accounts for 81.6% of all U.S. greenhouse gas emissions from human activity. CO_2 dominates the human gas emissions and, in 2016, the EPA reported that the combustion of fossil fuels to generate electricity was the largest single source of CO_2 emissions in the nation, accounting for about 34% of total U.S. CO_2 emissions and 28% of total U.S. greenhouse gas emissions.[8] Therefore it is unsurprising that there have been pressing demands to terminate the burning of fossil fuels for energy. Many people have turned to renewable energy sources: a key choice that will foster a big shrinkage in the output of future carbon dioxide emissions.

Methane (CH_4)

Methane — another greenhouse gas — arises from sources such as leaks of natural gas (in the gas industry), emissions from wetlands, and the raising of livestock. Generally, however, methane is associated with agriculture and farming. While some methane release into the atmosphere is from natural processes, such as the digestive processes of livestock, these levels increase beyond what the natural system can absorb as the scale of farming has increased and intensified. Moving into the future, the spread of agricultural land is bound to remain the same or decrease due to the climatic effects that will likely negatively impact food production (described in detail in Part II).

In 2016, methane (CH_4) accounted for about 10% of all U.S. greenhouse gas emissions from human activity.[9] Although this proportion is dramatically lower than that of CO_2, CH_4 is more efficient at trapping radiation than CO_2. Pound for pound, the comparative impact is more than 25 times greater than CO_2 over a 100-year period (GWP = 25).[9] Hence, CH_4 is a more potent greenhouse gas in terms of trapping solar radiation. This information is contrasted with some lighter news: methane only remains in the atmosphere for about a decade.[7]

Nitrous Oxide (N_2O)

Nitrous oxide is naturally present in the **nitrogen cycle** and is present as N_2 in 78% of Earth's atmosphere. Microbial transformations allow nitrogen to be used by plants, which ultimately sustains all animal life.[10] The specific causes of nitrous oxide emissions will be explored later in the chapter.

In 2016, the EPA found that nitrous oxide (N_2O) constituted about 6% of all U.S. greenhouse gas emissions from human activities.[9] This contribution is very small, but like methane, the GWP is extremely high. Specifically, the impact of 1 pound of N_2O on warming the atmosphere is almost 300 times that of 1 pound of carbon dioxide.[9] Moreover, N_2O remains in the atmosphere for 100 years.[7]

Greenhouse Gases by Economic Sector

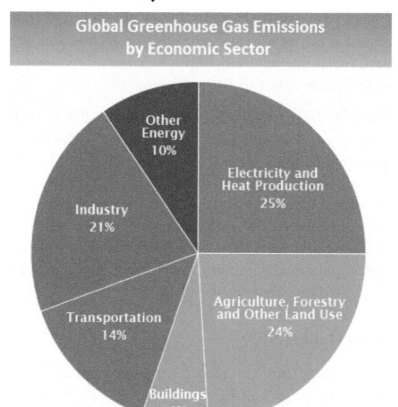

This pie chart by the EPA depicts the global distribution of GHG among various sectors. Courtesy of EPA.[11]

Following the discussion is about the four most abundant gases in the atmosphere. It is useful to learn of the **anthropogenic** causes of these greenhouse gases. The three main causes of the increase in greenhouse gases observed over the past 250 years have been fossil fuels, land use, and agriculture, as shown in the pie chart provided by the EPA.[9]

The sector contributing the highest to the total greenhouse gas emissions is the production of energy (i.e. electricity and heat) at 25%. Certain regions in the world still burn fossil fuels to create electricity. These nonrenewable resources contribute to major CO_2 emission, and energy production overall (heat and electricity) accounts for 25% of the increase.

In addition to energy production, 24% of emissions are attributable to AFOLU (agriculture, forestry, and other land use). The three greenhouse gases are released in three distinct ways when analyzing changes in land use. First, CO_2 releases are linked to deforestation, which contribute to 9% of CO_2 emissions.[12] As mentioned in the description of the gas, land sinks absorb more than half of carbon dioxide emitted by humans; thus, when forests are cut down, they release the stored CO_2 and thus contribute to warming.

Next, one CH_4 release factor is linked to the cultivation of rice. Having had the blessed opportunity to travel to Kerala (located in southern India), I witnessed the production of rice on a paddy field. The fields of green extended over large swaths of land in this region; they were manually constructed by humans to increase food production. However, I had no idea that they were in part contributing to 15-20% of the global methane emissions.[12] In fact, this clarifies the observations of the spike in atmospheric methane concentration 5000 years ago — the advent of farming was the cause.

Another major anthropogenic cause of methane emissions from AFOLU is farm animals/livestock. Approximately 37% of global methane emissions are somehow linked to the livestock, according to a 2006 UN FAO report.[12] More specifically, the digestive process of **enteric fermentation** in cattle releases methane through burping or farting. The third-leading cause for anthropogenic methane emissions is landfills, which contribute to roughly 18% of global methane emissions; this form of land use initially uses **aerobic decomposition**, but after only one year utilizes **methanogens** due to the lack of oxygen in the air.

Finally, the major cause of nitrous oxide emissions is fertilizer application for livestock, which is directly related to livestock on farmland. This contributes to 65% of global N_2O emissions.[12] Since the 1960s, the implementation of inexpensive, synthetic fertilizer to boost food production has coincided with a steep increase in N_2O emissions. This is due to the chemistry behind the fertilizer content. Specifically, the application of fertilizers stimulates microbes in the soil to convert N_2 to N_2O, bolstering atmospheric concentrations of nitrous oxide. Because N_2O's global warming potential is higher than that of CO_2 (carbon dioxide) and CH_4 (methane), many scientists believe that reducing N_2O emissions from fertilizer applications are of paramount importance. In the wise words of UC Berkeley chemistry professor Kristie Boering, "limiting N_2O emissions can buy us a little more time in figuring out how to reduce CO_2 emissions." [13]

The third-highest source of greenhouse gas emissions is industry. More precisely, the extraction and burning of massive amounts of fossil fuel (i.e., coal, oil) for industrial purposes is responsible for about 1/5th of the increase in release of gases. This helps to establish that nearly half of greenhouse gas emissions are directly related to the burning of fossil fuel and also explains the high proportion of carbon dioxide emissions (81%) compared to other gases.

Also worth mentioning is the burning of fossil fuels for transportation (14%) such as cars, planes, and trains (refer to diagram above). Moreover, the generation of heat in buildings (6%) accounts for smaller, but still significant, percentages that contribute to the overall increase in greenhouse gases.

Emissions by Country

As the causes of global warming and levels of greenhouse gas output vary significantly from country to country, there is no simple way to offer a solution to climate change. Therefore, the problem must be broken down into smaller parts, such as countries and regions, to examine how they each one emits greenhouse gases. The worldwide distribution of greenhouse gas emissions is heavily influenced by nations that are the most populous and industrialized — a combination which leads to them being major emitters of greenhouse gases.

As the upcoming and younger generation, we should aim to solve this problem in our lifetimes. For this to be the case, we must recognize and analyze the ways in which these countries are emitting greenhouse gases (i.e., industry and agriculture) so we can generate ways to reduce the emissions. Below are the four countries with the highest greenhouse gases emissions in the world.

China

By country, China is responsible for the most greenhouse gas emissions (roughly 10 billion tons of CO_2 alone), the highest CO_2 emissions (accounting for 30% worldwide), and the most coal production and consumption in the world (3.97 billion tons of coal were consumed by China in 2015).[14] This clearly points to the country's reliance on the burning of fossil fuels for energy. Since 2011, however, the percentage of coal used in total energy consumption in China has decreased from 70.2% to 62.0%.[14] China is definitely heading in the right direction towards renewable energy, but that is counteracted with an unfortunate statistic: there has been an increase in greenhouse gas emissions from energy consumption (power generation, heat, transportation) by 4% from 2011 to 2015.[15] This raises the question of what aspects of the Chinese economy continue to increase greenhouse gas emissions, if not coal consumption. One plausible explanation involves a shift in energy reliance from coal to other fossil fuels (i.e. oil and/or gas). Rather than solving the problem, turning to other nonrenewable sources of energy is avoiding the problem. Thus, burning fossil fuels for energy consumption contribute to disproportionately large emissions with regards to CO_2.

AFOLU (agriculture, deforestation, and other land use) accounts for more than 15% of China's total greenhouse gas emissions, nearly 90% of its nitrous oxide emissions, and 60% of its methane emissions.[16] The excessively high nitrous oxide and methane emissions are driven largely by excessive fertilizer use for livestock and the digestive processes of cattle themselves, respectively.

Additionally, some sources of greenhouse gas emissions in China cannot simply be altered due to their significance to the Chinese culture, namely rice. Understanding the value of rice in Asian culture is best cultivated through a historical lens, in spite of paddy field methane emissions. Tracing the symbolic significance of rice in Chinese cuisine, the ancient civilizations flourished adjacent to the Yellow and Yangtze Rivers. These river valleys provided fertile land and ideal farming conditions to establish a food surplus. Ever since those days, rice has played an integral role in the lives of all Chinese and South Asian nations. Without a doubt, this piece of Chinese culture will always remain; despite the greenhouse gas emissions released from rice cultivation, the identity of the Chinese is far more important. Nevertheless, methods of rice cultivation should be improved to mitigate CH_4 release.

In projections for the future, the Chinese should aim to drop the excessive emissions on energy production since this sector is contributing the most to the skyrocketing human emission activity. Their recent attempts to reduce coal usage and replacing it with renewable energy sources are commendable. However, they must continue this laudable mission until their emissions have reached extremely low quantities; only then will humanity make progress to reach the lowest emissions scenario and thus minimize the damage to Earth.

U.S.

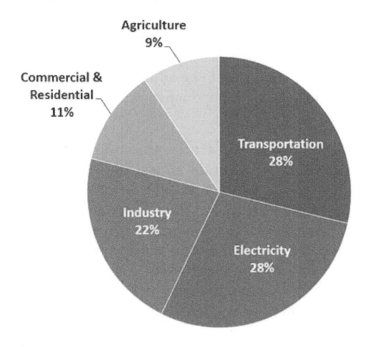

This pie chart details the distribution of GHG among sectors within the United States. Courtesy of the EPA.[17]

The U.S. is the second-highest emitter of greenhouse gases worldwide and is responsible for about 15% of total greenhouse gas emissions (over 5 billion tons of CO_2 alone).

The above diagram by the EPA depicts that transportation (the use of cars, ships, trucks, planes) releases carbon dioxide; over 90% of all fuels are still diesel and gasoline.[17] This proportion of total greenhouse gas emissions (28%) is exactly double the worldwide average (14%), as seen in the diagram above. This can be explained by the heavy traffic and extreme dependence on cars for all transportation, in contrast to a greater dependence on public transportation in other developed countries (e.g.,. European nations). In regards to U.S. transportation, American culture fuels both the love and obsession for cars, propelling more traffic in society. Few solutions currently exist, but among them are Elon Musk's Tesla Inc. This company seeks to spark a new market for cars: one of clean energy and zero carbon dioxide emissions. Furthermore, the new hybrid market is evidence of a changing preference towards renewable energy in transportation. Moving forward, the U.S. must continue on this excellent path towards providing high-quality transportation without releasing greenhouse gas.

Alongside transportation, electricity generates the largest share of greenhouse gas emissions in the United States; 68% of all electricity is still generated from coal and natural gas, which leads to the release of many greenhouse gases in the process.[18] Although many reformative measures have led to the clean generation of energy, the United States must continue to terminate the generation of electricity from burning fossil fuels and instead implement new renewable solutions across the nation. On a similar note, the electricity/power/energy industry is still very largely based on the burning of fossil fuels, leading to more greenhouse gas emissions. Within homes/businesses, fossil fuels generate heat and other forms of energy, and the handling of waste also contributes to greenhouse gases.[17] All in all, the majority of all U.S. greenhouse gases are driven by burning fossil fuels.

The remainder of emissions from the U.S. are derived from agricultural activities such as livestock and rice production (9%).[17] The exact causes are the same as those described in the previous section. In the past discussions of the AFOLU sector, however, we excluded its ability to absorb CO_2. In fact, this sector absorbs more CO_2 than it emits (i.e. net sink). But for the purposes of simplicity, total calculated greenhouse gas emissions do not include any absorption of CO_2 from the AFOLU sector. So when analyzing any data associated with greenhouse gas emissions, be sure to remember that there are some net sinks that are removing a small portion of these daunting numbers. Overall, a look at the United States demands a push for clean energy and moving away from the burning of fossil fuels.

Russia

The Russian Federation has seen a great dip in greenhouse gas emissions since the dissolution of the Soviet Union: from about 2.5 billion tons of CO_2 emissions in 1990 to 1.65 billion tons in 2012.[19] Nevertheless, it is ranked 4th in greenhouse gas emissions in the world. This high number is further analyzed by the Climate Action Tracker — an independent scientific assessment produced by three research groups that tracks climate pledges and policies. Based on Russian 2030 projected targets, this analysis found Russia's projections to be "critically inadequate." Specifically, its targets for greenhouse gas emissions, which include the following:

- 15-25% below 1990 levels (currently 33% below)

- 50% below 1990 levels by 2050.[19]

These numbers suggest very slow mitigation of Russian greenhouse gas emissions and offer little hope for dramatic improvement. By breaking down the economic sectors and their contributions to total greenhouse gas emissions, we will be able to thoroughly analyze how this massive yet sparsely populated nation ranks among the highest for emissions. In 2012, the distribution of greenhouse gas emissions by sector in Russia was as follows:

- 82% from energy sources (includes transportation, energy industries, manufacturing, and construction).

- 8% from industry (metallic and chemical processes, and production of halocarbons and SF_6).

- 9.5% from agriculture (majority agricultural soils, some manure and enteric fermentation, and very little rice production in Russia).[19]

Similar to the United States, Russia has a low priority of agriculture due to its unfavorable climatic conditions. Burning fossil fuels for energy and industrial manufacturing contribute in large part to these emissions. Moving towards the future, limiting the amount of fuel generated from fossil fuels will be critical for Russia and the world. In spite of the country's high rank, the major drop from 1990 offers hope following the end of the nuclear Cold War era.

India

The Indian economy saw a rise in CO_2 emissions in 2016 (4.7%), and another 4.6% in 2017 (now about 2.4 billion CO_2 tons).[20] These CO_2 emissions are largely due to the developing status of the country as it firmly establishes its role as an industrial, exporting powerhouse. Throughout the nation, emissions had previously increased 45% over a 10-year period (from 2000-2010).[20] However, Prime Minister Modi has pledged under the Paris Climate Agreement that by 2030 emissions will be 33-35% below 2005 levels. This can be achieved through the country's continued strategy for reducing greenhouse gas levels. More specifically, its efforts to minimize greenhouse gas emissions have been applied through the National Electricity Plan, which represents the government's effective efforts to make a measurable difference in emissions. The Plan was created in light of the booming economy and growing population, and the need to offset the effects in terms of global warming.

Breaking down the economic sectors and their contributions to greenhouse gas output, the distribution of greenhouse gas emissions in India is as follows:

- 71% Energy

- 18% Agriculture

- Methane (CH_4) due to livestock (enteric fermentation and manure management) & rice cultivation

- Nitrous oxide (N_2O) emitted through fertilizers applied to agricultural soils

- 8% industry

- Mineral, chemical, metallic production, non-energy (waxes and lubricants)

- 3% Waste (wastewater & solid waste disposal) [20]

To highlight just some problems that India faces as a nation in terms of reducing its greenhouse gases: India has the world's largest cattle population and thus a high level of emissions from agriculture (as high as 18%, as listed earlier). Other issues include that the energy network is still being rolled out in order to reach all corners of rural India (promoting industrialization), and that is that coal is abundant, cheap, and widely available, which keeps it as a the mainstay of energy in the country. Nevertheless, the aforementioned intentions to minimize greenhouse gas emissions prove to offer hope for the world, in addition to the ground-breaking Paris Climate Agreement (discussed later in Part I).

CHAPTER 3

POLITICIZATION

After having explored the technical situation of global warming, it is only realistic to recognize its place in the fiery political sphere. This chapter of Part I aims to detect the role of big business in climate change policy.

In the course of history, businesses have had periods in which they have thrived or plummeted, depending on many factors such as demand, the market, and access to necessary goods. Before climate change was fully recognized in recent years as a severe threat to the Earth, some businesses carelessly attained revenue by any means even if that meant emitting greenhouse gas into the atmosphere (i.e. burning fossil fuels). However in this day and age, with global warming right around the corner, it is time for business to meet social responsibility and truly follow environmental regulation in any undertaking. In that same vein, the deep connection between high-profile businesses and politics will be interrogated in this chapter — namely, the practice of lobbying.

Let me first define lobbying before we delve in. **Lobbying** is an effort:

* By which individuals or private interest groups attempt to influence the actions/decisions of the government.

* By which people with more leverage and power attempt to influence public policy.[21]

Lobbying is typically practiced by big businesses and wealthier individuals. This fact may be the reason the term has developed a negative connotation. Corporations sometimes try to slide past the rules, and many corporations have lobbied against policies that support climate regulations. However, lobbying is also practiced by those who have sought, and seek, to support climate regulations though a disproportionately large number of companies do actively opposed climate policy.

Many may wonder which businesses, and to what extent said businesses, advocate their personal position on climate policy. InfluenceMap, a U.K. non-profit organization, provides a database that intends to accurately represent corporations' responses to climate policy. In their September 2017 report, InfluenceMap tracked down the 250 largest public industrial companies and investigated their position on climate policy. The main lines of inquiry upon which the report was based included:

- Whether each corporation's policies were aligned with or against the Paris Climate Agreement's effort to combat climate change.

- To what extent the corporation's policies supported the position of the Paris Climate Agreement's effort to combat climate change.

- Whether the corporation had political power and how this affected the economic success of a company.

According to this report, of the "50 corporations across the world with the most extreme scores, 35 of them actively oppose climate policies while only 15 advocate climate policy" (shown below).[22] The rest of the 200 companies maintain a neutral stance. This current dynamic between business and climate policy presents a plethora of issues due to the threats of climate change.

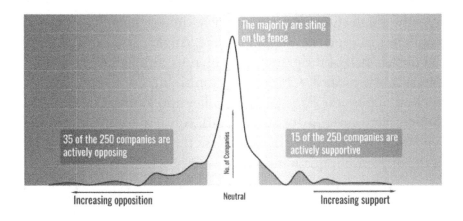

This illustration depicts the companies' position on climate change policy. Courtesy of InfluenceMap.[22]

As depicted above, the results showed that the majority of political activity was neutral, constituting about 80% of major international businesses. However, the extremities (i.e. the least supportive of climate policy or most supportive of climate policy) were extremely unequal. The vast majority of companies that decided to take a stance chose to oppose the climate policy (70% of non-neutral companies). Moving towards the future, as the next generation becomes the driving force in commerce, we must shift this majority towards support for climate policy for the sake of planet Earth. A shift in the stance of businesses would not only raise awareness for the phenomenon, but also prevent greenhouse gas emissions from commercial sources themselves.

Furthermore, another graph depicts companies and their specific stances relative to one another. This similar analysis compares companies' support for climate policies to their engagement intensity whether it's positive or negative. As shown below, the general trend creates a U-shaped curve where the majority of political action takes place under two circumstances: first, if the corporations actively oppose the Paris Climate policy or second, if the corporations are advocates of the policy.[22]

This thorough study finds ambitiously climate-friendly company names in the upper-right quadrant (i.e. Apple, Tesla, and IKEA). On the left-half of the graph are numerous companies in the utilities sector (i.e. Shell, Chevron, ExxonMobil, Southern Company) that oppose the Paris Climate policy and lobby against it. Although there currently exists this stark contrast, as the upcoming generation we should work to increase the number of companies in the upper right quadrant.

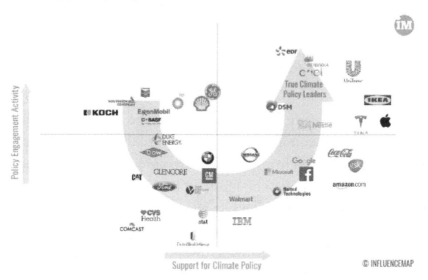

This graph displays the relationship between political engagement and support for climate policy. Courtesy of InfluenceMap.[22]

The company with the least support for climate policy is Koch Industries, owned by the influential and extremely rich Koch brothers. The company's holdings include a refinery and processor (for raw materials such as fossil fuels [including oil, ethanol, and natural gas]). The brothers are politically active against climate change regulation and, to date, have donated millions of dollars to defeat congressmen who want to take action against climate change. Since 1997, the Koch brothers have channeled $100 million to the promotion of climate change denial and in 2018 alone spent $5.6 million on lobbying for their desired lack of action.[23] This particular effort of climate lobbying is a setback from the groundbreaking 2015 Paris Climate Agreement, and truly influences the political sphere in Congress. As the younger generation, it is our duty to stop big businesses from exerting their power and influence over representatives in Congress. This form of action should be restricted instead of solely relying on morality and good judgment to encourage Congress to pass these climate regulations.

Sharing in Koch Industries, Shell, Chevron, and ExxonMobil lobbied $4 million, $5.6 million, $5.9 million, respectively, in 2018 alone.[23] These numbers, provided by the Center for Responsive Politics (a non-profit, nonpartisan research group that tracks the effect of money and lobbying on actual governmental legislation) offer proof of the destructive presence of big business not only on climate regulation policies, but also on any legislative, governmental action. Additionally, these three companies are among the top five highest companies that lobby on behalf of the oil and gas industries. This staunch opposition to climate policies needs to subside as our generation takes on the mantle of the business world, but that responsibility is on us.

Lobbying and greenhouse gas Emissions By Sector

It is important to note the actual greenhouse gas emissions for U.S. companies by sector. This will help clarify a connection between greenhouse gas emissions and climate lobbying. Below are, in ascending order, the amount of greenhouse gas emissions by sector and, in no particular order, the percentage of corporations that have lobbied against climate change policies:

- About 40% of corporations in the basic resources sector (which includes refinery and processing of raw materials in industries such as mining) lobbied against action on climate change. On average, this sector releases 25 million tons of CO_2 per year.

- Over 30% of corporations involved in the automobile industry are engaged in climate lobbying (cars that run on petrol release carbon dioxide). On average, this sector releases 39 million tons of CO_2 per year.

- 60% of corporations in the utilities sector are engaged in climate lobbying. On average, this sector releases 40 million tons of CO_2 annually).

- 22% of oil and gas corporations are involved in climate lobbying. This sector is responsible for the release of over 55 million tons of CO_2 greenhouse gases on average per year. It is also notable that the variance of greenhouse gas emissions among oil and gas corporations is 82 millions of CO_2. This emphasizes the high emissions of certain companies in the industry such as ExxonMobil, which emits over 300 million tons of CO_2 in a year.[24]

These numbers from a study published in the *Academy of Management Discoveries* demonstrate the high involvement of these sectors in climate lobbying.[24] We must ensure that serious action is taken by the U.S. government to mitigate the role of big business in climate change rather than allowing our representatives to be 'paid off' in various ways by those with vested interests, as seen from the study by InfluenceMap above. It is interesting that the oil and gas corporations release the most greenhouse gas, but in turn only 22% of them are involved in climate lobbying. Nevertheless, certain corporations like ExxonMobil release over 300 million tons of CO_2 in a year (putting this into perspective, the entire United States releases 5 billion tons of CO_2).[24]

This study affirmed that there exists a U-shaped distribution between the amount of greenhouse gases and political lobbying on climate policy. This indicates that the oil and gas/utilities/basic resources sector-based companies want to avoid costly regulation and lobby against climate policy while pro-environmental groups with clean energy policies are likely to support climate policy through lobbying (shown on the graph on the next page).

FIGURE 3
Graph of relationship between greenhouse gas
(GHG) emissions and lobbying expenditure

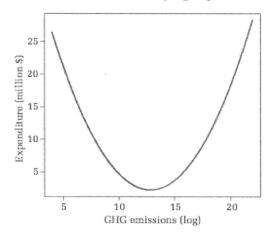

This graph above depicts the relationship between lobbying expenditure and GHG emissions as a U-shaped curve. Credit to Academy of Management Discoveries.[24]

All in all, this paints the extremes of the governmental debate on the issue: not as a partisan divide, but instead due to the destructive presence of business. Moving forward, our generation ought to amend the wrongs of past businesses and set forth in a climate-friendly manner in regards to both actually diminishing greenhouse gas emissions and public support for climate policy.

PART II

EARTH EFFECTS

Rising Temperatures, Sea Level Rise,
Ocean Acidification, Extreme Events

CHAPTER 4

RISING TEMPERATURES

B ehold, an Earth controlled by a natural climate is now in the past. Burning fuels to the extent that we have has given birth to a new era: one of globally **rising temperatures**.

The direct implication of global warming – the literal warming of the Earth on land – is clearly explained in this chapter. As explained in Part I, the nature of the greenhouse effect is that the greenhouse gases trap solar energy (that should ordinarily return to space) in the Earth's atmosphere. This means that the higher the quantity of greenhouse gases in the Earth's atmosphere, the higher the mean global temperature of planet Earth will become.

Here is some of the direct evidence, as given in the International Panel on Climate Change 2013 report:

By both the National Aeronautics and Space Administration (NASA) and National Oceanic and Atmospheric Administration (NOAA) analyses, 17 of the 18 warmest years since modern record-keeping began have occurred since 2001. "In summary, it is certain that globally averaged near-surface temperatures have increased since the late 19th century. Each of the past three decades has been warmer than all the previous decades in the instrumental record, and the decade of the 2000s has been the warmest." [1] More than 90% of the excess energy absorbed by the climate system since at least the 1970s has been stored in the oceans, which can be seen in global records of ocean heat content going back to the 1950s.[1]

Since the ocean heats up if, and only if, the climate system absorbs excess heat, land surface temperatures will likely increase at a faster rate than ocean temperatures. Increases in average global temperatures are expected to be within the range of 0.5°F to 8.6°F by 2100 with a likely increase of at least 2.7°F for all scenarios except the one representing the most aggressive mitigation of greenhouse gas emissions.[1]

The IPCC also reported that 2.7 degrees Fahrenheit could be reached in as little as 11 years—and almost certainly within 20 years without major cuts in carbon dioxide (CO_2) emissions. Even if such cuts were to begin immediately it would only delay, not prevent, 2.7 degrees Fahrenheit of global warming.[1]

Changes in daily human labor

The knock-on effects of climate change are multifaceted. The following reports point out how our daily working lives will be impacted by a rise in temperatures:

The International Panel on Climate Change 2014 edition released a statement of high confidence that the, "combination of high temperature in some areas for parts of the year is projected to compromise normal human activities... or working outdoors." [1]

According to a new NOAA study, heat-stress-related labor capacity losses will double globally by 2050 with a warming climate. These health-effects are further explained in Part III.[25]

At the moment, the hottest summer days limit us to 90% labor capacity. This is projected to decrease to 80% by 2050, and to as low as 40% by 2200 depending on the extent of CO_2 emissions.[25]

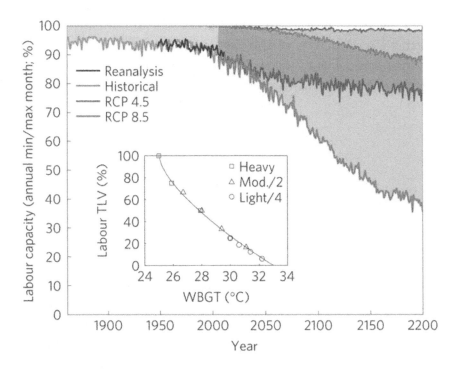

The graph above highlights the decline in labor capacity as temperature increases. Credit to Nature Climate Change.[25]

If these scientifically-based projections prove correct, greater chunks of the summer will be intolerable and at some point in the future our outdoor life will be restricted, as the human body is simply not built for such conditions. The changes are gradual, but will be kicking in decade after decade.

Adapting our behavior will be crucial to: 1) minimizing greenhouse gas emissions, and 2) supporting life within a new climate.

As long as temperatures continue to rise, humankind can be certain that greenhouse gases will be far too dominant in the atmosphere. We must take heed of the temperatures and statistics shown by scientific monitoring; they need to be given centre stage and positioned as humanity's wake-up call before more dramatic changes can manifest.

Stopping extra heat from being absorbed and trapped in the Earth's atmosphere is of the utmost importance both now and for the future. The resulting progress can be tracked by monitoring the degrees by which the temperature rises or, hopefully, fall.

CHAPTER 5

SEA LEVEL RISE

Sea level rise is a natural consequence of general temperatures rising, as touched on in the previous section.

Delving deeper, temperature rises contribute to sea levels or the expansion of ocean waters in a number of ways. The first is that warm sea water has a greater volume than cold sea water due to greater movement of molecules. The second is that rising temperatures cause mountain glaciers and ice caps to melt. For example, portions of the Greenland and Antarctic ice sheets would continue to melt at a faster rate and flow into the ocean.[26]

Thermal Expansion

As the oceans' waters heat up from CO_2 uptake, they act as a sink (absorption) for CO_2 causing the water to warm and, consequently, glacial melt. The resulting increase in all of the oceans' volumes leads to sea level rise. This is **thermal expansion**.

It has been calculated that for every degree Celsius that the ocean water warms, the resulting thermal expansion will contribute to nearly half a meter of sea level rise.

While thermal expansion in relation to the melt of small glaciers is relatively well-known, the much larger Antarctic and Greenland ice sheets are now being studied. Here are some of the findings to date:

- A large glacier in the East Antarctic Ice Sheet (EAIS) is as vulnerable to melting as the West Antarctic Ice Sheet (WAIS)

- Greenland and Antarctic edges are now susceptible to warmer waters, leading to melting at the tips.

- Antarctica is melting three times as fast as 10 years ago; this will contribute 6 inches to sea level rise by 2100.

The **Gulf Stream** is another important component to understand when thinking about the climate. The Gulf Stream refers to natural currents in the ocean that transport warm waters from the Tropics to the North Atlantic and back again, and play a large role in regulating the world's climate. Due to the warming of the ocean, this system is at its weakest point in over a thousand years. This weakening circulation is thought to play a major role in changing weather patterns and sea-level rise. However, that exact role is still uncertain to many scientists. For instance, some possible effects include swinging temperatures, hurricanes, and ocean levels, which is suggestive of extreme fluctuations in weather, rather than an overall trend or pattern such as increasing temperatures.

The Assessment Report 5 from IPCC concludes that across all **representative pathway concentrations** (all possible trajectories for CO_2 emissions and therefore the specific degree of sea level rise), the minimum sea level rise will be 9 inches and the maximum 32 inches by the late-21st century. In assessing the exposed populations, the majority of Southeast Asia is at highest risk for the rising waters, including nations such as Vietnam, Japan, and China.[26]

For the majority of the projected roughly 3 feet of sea level rise, scientists have predicted the connection to the glacial melt of the Greenland and Antarctic ice sheets by the year 2100.[26]

Coastal Populations

Sea level rise will hit coastal populations the hardest. It is expected that by 2060 there will be 1.3 billion people living in low-coastal zones (<10 meters above sea level). Sea level rises will lead to populations having to leave their homes and livelihoods to move further inland. Just as increasing temperatures will impact human lives, so will the changes that go hand-in-hand with this such as the rise in sea levels.

It is already certain that the waters will submerge cities like Miami, Florida; it is just a matter of when it will happen. How will I adapt from the life I know to another kind of life? Why does this problem have to happen in the first place? Why has our generation been dealt this blow by the cumulative actions of those who came before us?

Islands are most vulnerable to rises in sea level. Paul Kench, a geomorphologist at the University of Auckland, believes that many natural islands not touched by humans will be fine, due to their ability to, "change shape and move around to shifting sediments: growing in size, not shrinking." [27]

However, areas transformed by human development, such as the Maldives, cannot adapt to sea level rise and, as a result, are very vulnerable.

Another Scenario: Egypt

This ancient kingdom, and now country, has been dependent on the Nile and its fertile banks for over four millennia.

Due to rising sea levels, saltwater intrusion poses a great threat to the agriculturally rich Nile delta, which is responsible for the food supply of 80 million Egyptians.

Besides the literal and dangerous implications of this sea level rise, such damage would serve as a cultural breaking point for Egypt since the Nile delta is not just a food source, but also a cultural symbol for Egypt. Mahmoud Medany, a researcher at Egypt's Agricultural Research Center, spoke to *The New York Times* in 2013, saying, "The Nile is the artery of life, and the Delta is our breadbasket. And if you take that away, there is no Egypt." [28]

Let's look in further detail at the astounding implications for the globe if humans don't radically alter their course.

CHAPTER 6

OCEAN ACIDIFICATION

O cean acidification refers to the process in which the **acidity** of the ocean increases (the **pH** is lowered). For the most part, ocean acidification is caused by emissions of CO_2 related to human activity, so that will be our primary focus.

When excess CO_2 is absorbed from the atmosphere by the ocean, the combination of carbon dioxide and water leads to a series of chemical reactions, as shown in the chemical equations below:

1. $CO_2 + H_2O \rightarrow H_2CO_3$ (Carbon dioxide + Water → Carbonic Acid)

   In chemical reaction (1), the water from the ocean and extra carbon dioxide in the atmosphere combine to create carbonic acid. This compound has two hydrogen (H) molecules that can be dissociated and increase acidity.

2. $H_2CO_3 \rightarrow H^+ + HCO_3^-$ (Carbonic Acid → Hydrogen Ion + Bicarbonate)

   In chemical reaction (2), carbonic acid breaks down and loses one hydrogen atom, forming the bicarbonate compound. This increase in the hydrogen ion concentration leads to a higher degree of acidity in the ocean.

3. $HCO_3^- \rightarrow H^+ + CO_3^{2-}$ (Bicarbonate → Hydrogen Ion + Carbonate)

   In chemical reaction (3), the second hydrogen atom is taken from the bicarbonate, simply becoming carbonate. Here, bicarbonate functions as an acid and a hydrogen atom is stripped from the compound. This effectively drops the pH level, and completes the process of ocean acidification.

This leads to an increase in the hydrogen ion concentration, which rapidly increases the acidity of the ocean (defined as a drop in the pH). In other words, there is a positive correlation between the amount of CO_2 emitted and the acidity of the ocean.

One historical example of devastation caused by ocean acidification is the **Permian-Triassic Mass Extinction**. Occurring about 252 million years ago, this incident was the result of a major pulse of carbon dioxide emissions which, in turn, caused rapid acidification of the oceans.[32]

Over the last 250 years, the oceans have absorbed 560 billion tons of CO_2, increasing the acidity of surface waters by 30%. The estimates of future atmospheric and oceanic carbon dioxide concentrations indicate that, by the end of this century, the average surface ocean pH could be lower than it has been for more than 50 million years.[29]

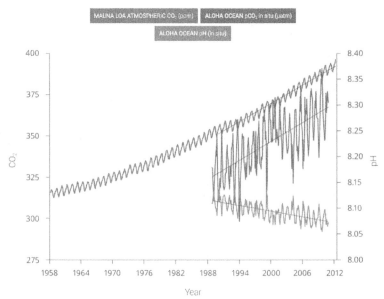

This graph depicts the trends of CO2 concentration and pH levels. Courtesy of JC Orr.[30]

Projections indicate that in higher emissions pathways the pH could be reduced from the current level of 8.1 to as low as 7.8 by the end of the century.[30]

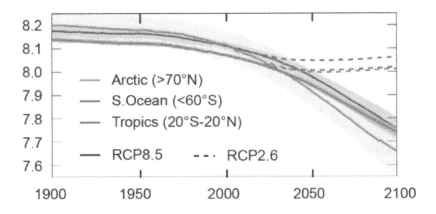

Above is a daunting projection of the acidity of sea levels due to ocean acidification. Credit goes to the IPCC 2014 report.[1]

So, what's the effect of ocean acidification? As a matter of fact, the phenomenon can largely disrupt marine life and ocean ecosystems due to the reduction in the concentration of carbonate ions, which are important for marine calcifying animals (zooplankton, mollusks, and shellfish) that form the basis of the marine food chain:

Here are a just a few of the sobering facts related to ocean acidification and its effects the food chain:

1. Ocean acidification jeopardizes coastal areas and seafood across the globe; more than a billion people today depend on the ocean for protein.

2. In what's termed "The Great Oyster Crash" of 2007, millions of oyster larvae died due to ocean acidification. More specifically, the oysters were unable to build their shells. This had a large knock-on effect on the U.S. oyster industry that year and is a 'warning sign' not only for the oyster

industry, but also — of course — for the ocean's overall ecosystem.

3. If CO_2 keeps rising at current rates, ocean acidification could slow coral growth by nearly 50% in 2050.[11] Coral is home to a quarter of all marine life, and fish that live and grow on coral reefs are a significant food source for about 500 million people.

Another important issue related to ocean warming involves the ability of the ocean to act as a 'carbon sink'. For millennia, the oceans have been absorbing carbon dioxide from the atmosphere.

As the ocean warms, the warmer ocean becomes less dense as the water molecules spread out. This results in **ocean stratification**, which is a big difference in density between the upper ocean and the intermediate and deep ocean.

With this increase in separation from the deeper ocean, the surface ocean will not mix with the ocean's deeper layers in the way that it typically would. Normally, the ocean's natural system would transport greenhouse gases such as CO_2 to deeper layer, but with the more concentrated stratification, more of the CO_2 remains in the upper layer. Due to the surface already carrying CO_2 volume up to maximum capacity, this leads to a reduction in ocean uptake of atmospheric CO_2. The natural cycle is further disrupted and atmospheric CO_2 levels are bound to increase.

Many leading scientists who are studying this issue have collaborated and predict that by 2100 the drop in oceanic uptake of CO_2 will be 30%.[29] Ocean acidification weakens the ability of the ocean to act as a sink, which in turn boosts global warming with higher concentrations of CO_2 in the atmosphere.

- For over 300 million years, the ocean's pH has stood at around 8.2, but since the industrial revolution the pH has dropped to 8.1. The danger is that, on its present course, the pH will continue dipping down to levels below that of

8: closer to a level of acidity that has not been experienced on earth for 50 million years.

- Marine life will be affected and certain locations in the U.S., particularly the Pacific Northwest, will be threatened as the shellfish industry will be particularly hard hit.

- Although ocean acidification is a less well-known consequence of global warming, the resulting threat to the marine ecosystem and disruption of the ocean's ability to act as a 'carbon sink' pose serious threats to life both in the ocean and on land.

CHAPTER 7

EXTREME EVENTS

Extreme weather events are defined as unexpected, unusual, or unseasonal weather by Intergovernmental Panel on Climate Change.

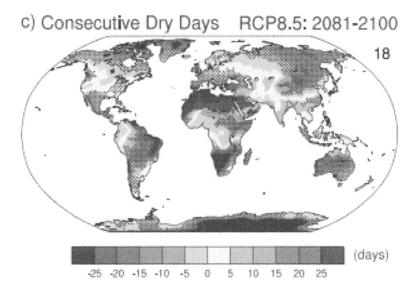

This potential projection of the Earth's dry days captures the increasing likelihood of extreme events. Credit to the IPCC.[1]

In most land regions, the frequency of warm days and warm nights will likely increase in the oncoming decades, while cold days and cold nights will decrease.

The above graph depicts the IPCC projection illustrating how the ratio between extremely hot days and extremely cold days will increase. By the end of this century, what had previously been once-in-20-year extreme heat days (1-day events) are projected to occur every two or three years over most of the U.S.[33] Humankind will have to adapt to hotter and hotter extremes becoming far more frequent.

Under higher emission scenarios, widespread drought is projected to become more common over most of the central and southern United States, and the frequency and intensity of heavy precipitation events over land will likely increase on average in the near term.[34] Scientific studies have shown that warmer surface temperatures are also associated with an increase in the intensity of hurricanes.

Fires

Throughout the state of California (specifically Northern California), there have been countless fires that have scorched and ravaged the lands,yielding extensive property loss and human fatality. The October 2017 firestorm was comprised of over 250 wildfires that consumed nearly a quarter million of acreage. Of these fires, the Tubbs fire grew to become the most destructive wildfire in the history of the state. Moreover, in 2018, the Mendocino Complex fire emerged as the second most destructive wildfire after the former from the previous year. The startling frequency of wildfires have begun to frighten the residents of California, as a fire can easily be sparked by worsening, dry conditions.

According to a report examining the ramifications of wildfires in Yellowstone by Proceedings of the National Academy of Sciences, the area burned by wildfires in North America is expected to increase dramatically over the rest of the 21st century due to climate change.[35] Wildfire seasons have become a much larger in size, more destructive, and longer in duration.

I have witnessed wildfires first-hand and seen fires rage in close proximity to my home in Southern California. Despite being only sixteen at the time of writing this book, I have even witnessed a change during my lifetime. Throughout my entire childhood, I remember only one major wildfire near my home, but in the past two years several wildfires have consumed land less than 5 miles away in the brushwood of nearby hills. Myself and several other young South Californians share sadness as the land of our childhood burns more frequently with every new year. The despairing truth is that a fire is able to sprout up at any time due to the increased length of droughts, lack of rainfall, and intensified heat affecting the state.

Aside from the ever-so-frequent infernos, another extreme event that is predicted to be exacerbated is rainfall. Although it might seem counterintuitive that global warming can cause an increase in rainfall, warming adds water vapor to the atmosphere,thereby causing wet areas to become even wetter.

Rain and Storms

A one degree Fahrenheit increase in temperature results in 4% increase in water-holding capacity and this, in turn, leads to more destructive and intense flooding. In addition to the immediate destructive impacts of flooding, a later consequence will likely be that more stagnant water could lead to various human health impacts, which will be discussed in Part III (i.e., contamination of water and water-borne disease).

Water flooding is also directly linked to the emergence of more storms, such as hurricanes. As explained by Columbia University's Applied Physics Professor Adam Sobel, "there's almost unanimous agreement that hurricanes will produce more rain in a warmer climate. There's agreement there will be increased coastal flood risk, at a minimum, because of sea level rise." [36]

Hurricanes are becoming more intense, due to their reliance on ocean warmth for strength; therefore global warming bolsters the intensity of the storm. Moreover when hurricanes operate in tandem with higher sea levels, this results in a greater storm surge, which is a major threat to the low coastal zones.

Scientific models project a slight decrease in the annual number of tropical cyclones by late this century, but an increase in the number of the strongest (Category 4 and 5) hurricanes. Explaining the gradual intensification of hurricanes, NASA Goddard Institute for Space Studies (GISS) scientist Timothy Halls claims that hurricanes could reach potentially reach wind speeds of up to 230 mph by 2100 due to warmer waters.[36]

A study by National Center for Atmospheric Research studied 20 Atlantic hurricanes and projected how these same storms would behave within the climatic conditions that are expected at the end of the 21st century. Their findings indicate that the hurricanes would generate an average of 24% more rain; such an increase suggests that such storms in the future will produce catastrophic flooding. Stronger, more intense storms will also result in more damage to infrastructure, leading to costlier losses.[37]

In its entirety, extreme events are expected to increase alongside the morbid trends of global warming. For example, very hot areas will be prone to intense droughts, coastal zones will be particularly affected by storm surges and hurricanes, and areas of high humidity, such as the tropics, could be subjected to more intense rainfall. Extreme events in a warming world will be continuously redefined and studied, and human adaptation as well as mitigation of root causes will be crucial to adapt to the effects of global warming.

If we gauge the likelihood of future scenarios based on current statistics and projections, loss of life due to global warming will increase dramatically throughout the rest of the 21st century, and our children and grandchildren will have to adapt to living in a harsher, unforgiving future climate.

The following Part will be dedicated to the exploration of the implications of catastrophic events on human health and how the overall trend of global warming will not only exacerbate. but also give rise to new health-related problems for humankind.

PART III

IMPLICATIONS ON HUMAN HEALTH

Heat stress, air pollution, water-borne
diseases, vector-borne diseases

CHAPTER 8

HEAT STRESS

In correlation with the discussion in Part II, the direct human health implications due to rising temperatures are as follows: based on present-day sensitivity to heat, by the end of the century an increase of thousands to tens of thousands heat-related deaths are projected each year as a result of climate change for the U.S. population alone.

The numbers for heat-related deaths are expected to increase while the number for cold-related deaths are projected to decrease (with a net increase in number of temperature-related deaths). The application of these results to "business as usual" climate predictions indicates that by the end of the century climate change will lead to increases of 3% in the age-adjusted mortality rate.[38]

Heat-related illnesses compromise the body's ability to regulate temperature and may lead to heat stroke. **Heat stroke** is caused by a core body temperature greater than 104 degrees Fahrenheit, with complications involving the central nervous system that occur after exposure to high temperatures.[39] The symptoms involve a progression from milder heat-associated illnesses such as heat cramps and exhaustion, and can then cause injury to the brain and other internal organs. It can even lead to death.

The symptoms of heat stroke range from nausea to confusion/disorientation, before giving way to loss of consciousness. The risk of heatstroke rapidly escalates when dealing with outside temperatures of 90 degrees or more, and the frequency of such extreme-temperature days are expected to increase with global warming. Prevention techniques include wearing light clothing, applying sunscreen, and drinking plenty of fluids.

One condition is primarily dependent on the temperature of the environment, which can thereby affect internal body temperature. Normally, the hypothalamus in the brain regulates body temperature and maintains homeostasis (the state of steady internal conditions) in the body. However, **hyperthermia** is classified as "elevated body temperature due to failed thermoregulation that occurs when a body produces or absorbs more heat than it dissipates." [40]

In other words, once in a state of hyperthermia, the body is no longer able to maintain homeostasis or control over its temperature. This leads to the body being unable to release heat from its system and, it instead absorbs heat from its surroundings, thus raising the body temperature far above normal. Hyperthermia can follow on from heat stroke which, as explained earlier in the chapter, is caused by excessive heat, and the symptoms can include heat cramps, heat stroke, heat exhaustion, and a deterioration into chronic conditions (including cardiovascular, respiratory, cerebrovascular and diabetes-related illnesses). [40]

In light of the rising temperatures and extreme events presented in Part II, the number of incidents of this condition occurring will undoubtedly become more frequent.

Climate change and global warming can also exacerbate chronic, non-communicable disease. When considering the impacts of global warming on health, these chronic conditions are often overlooked since the focus is often on vector-borne infectious diseases. A **chronic disease** is defined as one that lasts over 3 months, and is usually associated with prolonged illnesses in the elderly population.

One measurable way to determine the effect of heat-related illness on human health is to record the number of hospital admissions and emergency visits during extreme weather. One study published in the *American Journal of Respiratory and Critical Care Medicine* gives insight into the link between heat-related illness and human health. Specifically, it finds that, "each 10°F increase in daily temperature was associated with a 4.3% increase in same-day emergency hospitalizations for respiratory diseases."[41]

Another report recorded in the *Iranian Journal of Public Health* affirms a strongly positive correlation between extremely hot temperatures and cardiovascular disease. Conducting a case study in the Middle Eastern nation of Iran, researchers concluded that a 1°C increase in maximum daily temperature is associated with a 4.27% increase in cardiovascular disease mortality.[42]

In a study of the link between heat-related illness and renal failure, they found that when temperature acted as the only independent variable with all others constant, the amount of hospitalization increases. Published in the *American Journal of Epidemiology*, researchers performed a case-crossover study in New York, finding a correlation of "9% increase in odds of hospitalization for acute renal failure per 5°F (2.78°C) was found for mean temperature."[43] It is notable that although the study for renal disease only had a temperature change half that of the respiratory disease study, the likelihood of hospitalization was more than doubled. These dreadful statistics highlight the potent impact of temperature on human health, particularly on a multitude of human organs (i.e. lungs, kidneys, heart).

In an effort to glean some understanding about the kidney diseases, it may be wise to understand the scientific phenomena behind them. When kidney failure occurs, the kidneys cannot filter waste from the blood, which is their main function. Kidney failure is increased by climate change and a warmer environment.

Another renal problem is **kidney stones**, which are hard deposits made of minerals and salts that form inside the kidneys. These deposits cause urine crystallization due to the solidification of particles. Low intake of water leads to high concentration of urine and the risk of kidney stones, while drinking water leads to dilution of the urine, leading to less concentration of the salts.

The connection between climate and kidney stones was further explored in an investigation in 2011 by researchers Fakheri and

Goldfarb. Releasing their findings in *Kidney International,* the researchers determined that the amplification of climate change and the resultant impact of increased temperatures has been linked with kidney stone prevalence. This is explained through increased dehydration, thereby directly leading to concentration of the salts that form kidney stones. The study further projected the possible expansion of the regions that have increased kidney stones risk in a warmer future.[44]

Vulnerable populations

Particular groups within the population are more susceptible to heat-related illness:

- The Elderly population

  In individuals over the age of 65, there is a link between rising temperatures and the worsening of chronic conditions. In elderly people, the system within the body that regulates temperature becomes less effective, which can lead to a potential increase in respiratory and cardiovascular problems, and even death. The link between extreme climatic heat and rising hospital admissions of the elderly is well established.

- Children

  During heat waves children are more susceptible to dehydration, electrolyte imbalance (too much or too little calcium, sodium, and potassium), fever, renal disease, and hyperthermia. During infancy, the body is less effective at regulating its temperature and has a heightened metabolic rate during extreme heat. So, for example, if you want to participate in sports, such as playing on your high school football team, you are more at risk during heat waves due to the combination of physical exertion and raised temperature.

By recognizing the future of global warming as inevitable, these two age groups are certainly at the highest risk. However, *any* human body's ability to maintain internal homeostasis and a healthful balance of minerals is severely threatened by abnormal air temperatures. As the younger generation, we must work to protect first ourselves, followed by our future children who will have to learn to adapt and endure a hotter world.

Adaptation

Adaptation in this context refers to the means and tools for adapting to heatwaves, which include air conditioning, improved social responses, and acclimatization. Here are some of the factors to consider in relation to how our bodies and societies currently adjust, and furthermore how we increasingly need to adjust in the future:

- Physiological acclimatization: this refers to how our bodies automatically acclimatize in order to regulate body temperature, and includes changes in: sweat volume and timing, blood flow and heat transfer to the skin, and kidney function in hotter climates.

- Infrastructure changes, such as air conditioning in homes and businesses, public health programs, and appropriate healthcare.

The above are obvious examples of current methods of dealing with hot temperatures. As a young generation prepared to tackle this issue, it is our duty to find innovative solutions, such as heat sinks, to minimize the drastic effect of heat in the future.

While historically adaptation has outpaced warming, many studies project a future increase in mortality even when including assumptions regarding adaptation, as highlighted in this quote from a New York City climate change study in *American Journal of Public Health*: "the range of projections [the New York study has] developed suggests that by midcentury, acclimatization may not completely mitigate the effects of climate change ... which would result in an overall net increase in heat-related premature mortality." [45]

The New York study, focusing on its metropolitan population, projects that without considering acclimatization, there would be a 95% increase in heat-related mortality by 2050 compared to 1990s levels; however, only 25% of these projected deaths would be reduced by acclimatization, thus yielding a 70% increase in heat-related death by 2050. [45]

However, the above results may be exaggerated due to the following phenomenon. New York is particularly vulnerable as an **urban heat island**, meaning that it has higher heat due to the concentration of human activity and presence of man-made materials, such as concrete, that do not dissipate heat, and having fewer trees (which can help to regulate the heat). This concept of the "urban heat island" sets up New York as an extreme example of heat-related illness, and not representative of the majority of regions across the globe. Nevertheless, this study serves to indicate that adaptation may not fully outpace the temperature increase in the same way that it could in the past, leading to more fatalities.

As future generations of doctors and healthcare workers begin to assess the warming conditions of our environment, it is certain that the frequency of respiratory, circulatory, hormonal, urinary, genital, and renal diseases will spike. [46] This not only augments the urgent need for doctors and scientists to both continue high-quality treatment for the ill and develop sustainable solutions to heat-related illness, but also encourages many people (including myself) to potentially carve a pathway towards these careers from a moral outlook during the inevitable consequences of global warming. As I grow older, I hope to use these health revelations to partake in developing innovative solutions to the traditional field of medicine. Namely, this has conjured in me a deep and profound love for the field of biomedical engineering.

CHAPTER 9

AIR POLLUTION

Higher temperatures, including those caused by global warming, can intensify some types of air pollution such as **ground-level ozone**.

This type of ozone (O_3)—not to be confused with the ozone layer that absorbs the sun's UV radiation—occurs as a result of a chemical reaction between pollutants (emissions by cars, power plants, refineries and factories) and sunlight.

During the Great Smog of London, which occurred between December 5th and 9th, 1952, a heavy smog was responsible for over 10,000 deaths and caused nearly 100,000 people to become ill. The smog effects (comprised largely of ground-level ozone) on the human respiratory tract were devastating. Based on the phenomenon of rising temperatures, ozone levels are highly likely to increase as forecasted by many prominent studies such as the 2008 Royal Society Science Report. History may repeat itself with the current greenhouse gas emissions scenario due to the chemical formation of ground-level ozone and its exacerbation through global warming.

Ground-level ozone is formed just above the earth's surface in a reaction between two primary pollutants (nitrogen oxides and VOCs or **volatile organic compounds**) in sunlight and stagnant air. High temperatures are accompanied by less wind, leading to atmospheric stagnation. They also promote accelerated production of ozone since higher temperatures refer to higher activation energy and thus lead to more collisions between the two reactants.[47] The EPA diagram (shown below) details the formation of the reactants that create ozone and briefly presents the chemical process. This chemical understanding is further bolstered by data observations from studies, which will be presented below.

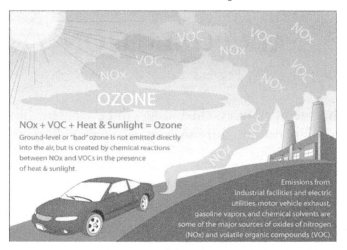

This diagram depicts the chemical and industrial factors that create ground-level ozone. Courtesy of the Environmental Protection Agency.[48]

As temperatures rise, the increase in ground-level ozone concentration goes up, proven by a multitude of credible studies. This graph on the right (again NYC so an urban heat island) confirms the positive correlation between ground-level ozone and rising temperatures.[49]

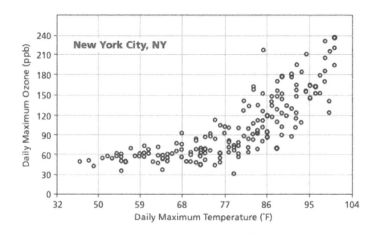

This graph highlights the positive correlation between ozone concentration and daily temperature highs. Courtesy of NAST.[49]

A further *Atmospheric Environment* study conducted by Jacobs and Winner in 2009 determined that the observed correlation between surface ozone and temperature in polluted regions points to a detrimental effect of warming. Using advanced atmospheric models, the researchers found that climate change alone will increase summertime surface ozone in polluted regions by 1–10 parts per billion over the coming decades, with the largest effects in urban areas and during pollution episodes.[50]

These statistics prove to be startling as there now exists a confirmed link between ozone levels and climate change. Studies of the health effects of ozone will now be explored.

Health effects

Climate-driven increases in O_3 will cause thousands of premature deaths per year as well as cause acute respiratory symptoms, as listed below.[51] The image below by *Sleep Aider* helps visually display some effects of ozone pollution on the human respiratory tract.

This illustration explains the symptoms of ozone inhalation on the human respiratory tract. Courtesy of SleepAider.[53]

Some of the immediate effects of dangerous levels of ozone include:

- Constriction of muscles in the airways, thereby trapping air and causing shortness of breath and wheezing.

- Inflammation and damage in the airways.[52]

According to a 2011 study by the Union of Concerned Scientists, a non-profit organization combining rigorous scientific analysis and citizen advocacy, higher ground-level ozone concentrations due to rising temperatures in 2050 could lead to an average of 11.8 million additional occurrences of asthma attacks, chest tightness, and shortness of breath.[53]

Additionally, the types of chronic respiratory diseases that can be aggravated due to an increase of ground-level ozone concentration are specified in the list below:

- Aggravation of lung diseases such as asthma, emphysema, and chronic bronchitis.

- Chronic obstructive pulmonary disease.

- Chronic genetic diseases such as asthma, which might be aggravated for life.

- Permanent lung damage (abnormal lung development in children).

- Overall damage to lungs and respiratory tract, affecting the ability to inhale oxygen forever.[52]

These lifelong impacts of ground-level ozone concentration prove to be extremely hazardous. In addition to all the symptoms above, a report by New England Journal of Medicine finds that there is a "significant increase in risk of death from respiratory causes in association with increase in ozone concentration."[55] If a person is sensitive to unhealthy air, it is imperative that they avoid major pollution, since ozone could be a major element in the smog; and as explained above, this is projected to be the case due to the clear link between rising temperatures and the destructive variant of ozone.

With this in mind, it is worth keeping track of the **Air Quality Index** (AQI) near you. The AQI is a very good indication of the levels of ozone pollution or fine particulate matter, allowing affected communities to distinguish between healthy and hazardous air. The next section in this chapter will inspect another major pollutant that can affect the human respiratory tract.

Wildfires

As previously mentioned, due to global warming there is an increase in frequency and duration of large wildfires and wildfire seasons in the western U.S.[35] These fires are catalyzed by dying vegetation, like grass and trees, which only continue to die out due to climate change conditions.

Wildfires are a major source of **fine particulate matter** (less than 2.5 micrometers in diameter, abbreviated PM) pollution, especially in the western U.S. in the summer. Particulate matter is an airborne pollutant that can arise either naturally or as a result of human activity, and can be made up of dirt, dust, smoke or liquid droplets. Chemically, these particles may be comprised of sulfates, nitrates, ammonium, organic carbon, and elemental carbon. In the case of wildfires, the resulting fine PM is carried downwind (along with the direction of the wind).

During the writing of this book and a few previous years, wildfires have conquered the headlines in the northern California region. To imagine that these horrendous events will increase is just mind-boggling. In November 2018, the Camp Fire blazed through Northern California leaving 76 casualties, making the inferno the deadliest in California history. As a result of this wildfire, the AQI has skyrocketed beyond 400 in some areas, where 50-100 is deemed normal. This is among the worst air quality in the entire world, making breathing extremely hazardous due to the high concentration of PM and ozone. Together, as the generation entering the workforce and becoming voters, we must learn the exact health effects of these blazes and begin to develop solutions to mitigate respiratory illness, such as more accessible N95 respirators or P100 masks.

Furthermore, in the connection between global warming and PM levels, there is no consensus yet on whether *meteorological* changes will lead to a net increase or decrease in fine particulate PM levels in the United States, although what is certain is that an increase in wildfires will lead to the creation of more PM.

In a study published in *Journal of Geophysical Research: Atmospheres*, researchers investigated the changes in carbon concentration within particulate matter by 2050. Their predictions reveal that wildfires in the western United States are, "projected to result in 40% increases of organic carbon and 20% increases in elemental carbon [particulate matter] concentrations." [56] These findings predict higher concentrations of particulate matter in wildfires in the future, suggesting a greater threat to human health as the number of wildfires are expected to steadily increase.

In Delhi, India, fine particulate levels have reached upwards of 999 on the Air Quality Index where over 500 is considered an emergency. This sprawling metropolis represents the worst of particulate matter levels and air pollution.

Health impacts

PM affects human health in many ways, leading to premature death and increased hospital visits. When humans breathe in air full of PM, the tiny toxic matter travels deep into the lungs and may even end up in the bloodstream, causing the various symptoms in human health.

The effects of fine PM (under 2.5 micrometers wide) on human health documented by the EPA are shown below and they are very similar to the effects of ground-level ozone pollution in that they can cause the following:

- Chronic obstructive pulmonary disease (COPD) with the symptoms culminating in overall chronic lung disease.

- Aggravation and development of asthma.

- Pulmonary inflammation and/or thombrotic responses.

- Activation of clotting pathways, enhancing the likelihood of an obstructive cardiac ischemic event (e.g., myocardial infarction) or cerebral event (e.g., stroke).[57]

Acute effects are likely that the progression of global warming and the resulting increases in levels of fine particulates in the atmosphere results in more cases of asthma. Asthmatic symptoms arise as a result of oxidative stress and inflammation of respiratory pathways.

- Provided by the National Heart Lung and Blood Institute, **asthma** is a "chronic lung disease that inflames and narrows the airways, which causes recurring periods of wheezing (a whistling sound when you breathe), chest tightness, shortness of breath, and coughing."

- More than 34 million Americans have been diagnosed with asthma.

- Asthma rates have increased from approximately 8–55 cases per 1,000 persons to approximately 55–90 cases per 1,000 persons between 1970 and 2000.[58]

The National Center for Health Statistics for U.S. Children provides some insight on the widespread impacts of asthma in the U.S. youth.

- Nearly 6.8 million children in the United States are affected by asthma, making it a major chronic disease of childhood.

- Asthma is also the main cause of school absenteeism and hospital admissions among children.

- In 2008, nearly 1 in 10 American children age 2 to 17 years were reported to have asthma.[59]

In all, the future is inevitably expected to see levels of ground-level ozone and wildfire frequency increase, thereby releasing hazardous particulate matter in the air, leading to detrimental effects on human health. Moving forward, seeking out solutions to shield the human respiratory tract from unhealthy air is likely the only option. Our air will gradually become more contaminated and future generations will be forced to take evolutionary, adaptive measures to preserve health worldwide.

CHAPTER 10

WATER-BORNE DISEASE

Increased temperature is linked with changes in geographic and seasonal growth of freshwater and marine toxin-producing harmful algae, as well as *Vibrio* bacteria (bacteria which are commonly found in certain coastal waters and exist in greater concentration as the water warms). This rapid accumulation of algal population in freshwater or marine ecosystems is known as **algal bloom** (shown below). Increased higher temperatures (>77 degrees Fahrenheit) favor cyanobacteria (harmful algae) over the harmless algae.

The picture above depicts the effect of increased water temperatures on algae, forming thick, pea-soup colored blooms. Courtesy of Dan Kraker.[60]

In turn, the increase in these kinds of harmful algae and bacteria leads to higher risk of waterborne pathogens (bacteria, viruses, and protozoa) and, therefore, to illnesses.

Exposure occurs through ingestion, inhalation, direct contact with contaminated water, and eating fish. Recreational activities in freshwater and marine water can also increase the risk of exposure to water-borne pathogens and toxins. More illnesses are related to freshwater exposure than to marine water exposure.

Additionally, enteric viruses from human waste that find their way into the water system through sewage discharge can cause gastrointestinal illness. Some Northeast and Great Lakes cities in the U.S. have combined sewer systems which discharge raw sewage into nearby surface waters. The result is a buildup of pathogens, drifting into surface waters (both freshwater and marine water).[61]

Effects on Health

- Harmful algal blooms create water-borne toxins. Symptoms from contact can include: rash, blisters, eye irritation, earache, wheezing, diarrhea, and vomiting.

- Water-borne pathogens are estimated to cause 8.5% to 12% of acute gastrointestinal illness cases in the United States, affecting between 12 million and 19 million people annually. Eight pathogens constitute 97% of all waterborne illnesses in the U.S.

- Bacterial pathogens (such as *Vibrio* species) may result in eye, ear, and wound infections, diarrheal illness, or death.

- Harmful algal blooms make up nearly half of all reported outbreaks in freshwater in 2009 and 2010.

- People with pre-existing respiratory illness like asthma are more at risk.[62]

In rural areas, and specifically on farms, many tons of manure are utilized by farmers for fertilization. Runoff from land where manure has been used can carry contamination from land to water; this runoff is increased by the intensity and frequency of flooding events.[63] Better manure application and management would reduce nutrients for harmful algal bloom and help eliminate water-borne illness agents.

In a study published by *Environmental Health Perspectives*, the researchers found that, "extreme precipitation events have been statistically linked to increased levels of pathogens in treated drinking water supplies and to an increased incidence of gastrointestinal illness in children."[64] This supports that global warming's cause of the increased frequency of extreme events has a direct correlation to water-borne illness due to the presence of more pathogenic organisms in the freshwater.

Furthermore, this connection between extreme events (flooding) and water-borne disease is bolstered by the following scenarios:

- The Milwaukee *Cryptosporidium* outbreak of 1993 was the largest documented water-borne disease outbreak in U.S. history. This event was preceded by the heaviest rainfall event in 50 years in adjacent watersheds. Rather than merely being attributed to coincidence, many investigations studying the incident have demonstrated a causal relationship.[65]

- Projections of more frequent or severe extreme precipitation events, flooding, and storm surge suggest that drinking-water infrastructure may be at greater risk of disruption or failure due to damage or exceedance of system capacity.

- According to a 2013 study published in the journal *Water Research*, *Salmonella and Campylobacter* (protozoa), concentrations in freshwater streams in the southeastern United States increase significantly in the summer months and following heavy rainfall.[66]

Algal toxins (harmful algal blooms) also have the ability to contaminate seafood as fish and other aquatic creatures interact with the floating algal groups. Instances of food poisoning from seafood are bound to increase due to harmful algal blooms, thereby affecting human digestion.

- CFP (Ciguatera Fish Poisoning) is the most frequently reported fish poisoning. There is a well-established link between warmer ocean temperatures and increased occurrences of CFP. "The projected 4.5°F to 6.3°F increase in sea surface temperature in the Caribbean over the coming century is expected to increase the incidence of ciguatera fish poisoning by 200% to 400%," as proven by a 2014 study analyzing the relationship between CFP and climate change.[67]

- PSP (Paralytic Shellfish Poisoning) is the most globally widespread shellfish poisoning associated with water-borne toxins. Its prevalence has also been linked with warmer temperatures , and there has been an increase in both PSP and ocean temperatures since the 1950s.

Populations at Risk

- Children, older adults, pregnant women, and immunocompromised people carry a higher risk of contracting a gastrointestinal illness.[68] Between 1997 and 2006, 40% of swimming-related eye and ear infections reported in children resulted from Vibrio alginolyticus bacterium.[69]

- Climate change will bring about an increase in seafood contamination by toxins. This is a particular risk for traditional, tribal Alaskan populations in the U.S. (which is 3-10 times higher in seafood consumption than the diet of the average U.S. population) and other places around the world whose populations depends on fish as part of their diet.[69]

CHAPTER 11

VECTOR-BORNE DISEASE

These illnesses refer to those that are caused by **vectors**, such as mosquitoes, ticks and fleas. These vectors carry infectious pathogens (parasites, bacteria, viruses) that are responsible for the actual disease.

Infectious diseases are bound to be prevalent throughout longer seasons because of more stagnant water areas from more extreme rainfall; therefore, they are able to extend their reach to new geographic locations.

Malaria

Some background information on the infamous disease includes the pathogen behind the "chilling fevers." The parasite known as *Plasmodium* is carried by female *Anopheles* mosquito, which lays eggs in water-filled containers. Some specific symptoms of malaria include initial acute febrile illness which worsens into fever, and causes headache and chills.[70] If people infected with the disease are not treated within 24 hours, it can lead to death.

In addressing the relationship between malaria and climate change, researcher Cyril Caminade of the University of Liverpool utilized models that, "show a consistent increase in the simulated [2050-modeled] length of malaria transmission season over the highlands at the regional scale. This can be seen over eastern Africa, South Africa, central Angola, the plateaux of Madagascar, Central America, southern Brazil, eastern Australia, and at the border between India and Nepal."[71] This list of regions are all at risk for a greatly-elongated season of malaria transmission due to climate change.

Furthermore, in a case study of certain West African regions, climate change was found to have the potential to instigate the spread of malaria in, "high altitude areas, particularly those with an altitude over 2,000m because lower regions are already sufficiently warm for the breeding of the mosquito vector." [72] One projection even involves malaria moving into the highlands of East Africa, an area where malaria has never existed. This specific demonstration of malaria spreading into new territory can be applied to other highlands across the globe, leading to a renewed ability for malaria to spread back into previously-eradicated or untouched areas.

High rates of illness and death occur when malaria reaches a non-immune population that has never experienced malaria. The map below shows the potential distribution of malaria parasite *Plasmodium falciparum* based on the Hadley Centre model's high-case scenario. Yellow indicates the current malaria distribution, while areas in red indicate the possible spread of malaria to areas where the climate will be ideal for the mosquitoes by the year 2050.

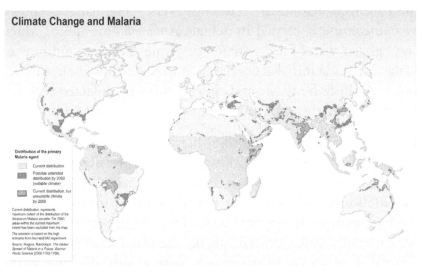

This map indicates the current and projected distribution of malaria across the globe. Courtesy of Hugo Alhenius from UNEP/GRID-Arenal.[73]

Rising temperatures and extreme events lead to a warmer and wetter tropical scenario, which is ideal for the *Anopheles* mosquito to thrive.

In a 2012 scientific study identifying the relationship between malaria transmission and patterns of rainfall due to the Indian Ocean Dipole (IOD), researchers determined that there is a positive association between malaria outbreaks and rainfall. This is probably because it creates many stagnant pools of water, which are fertile breeding grounds for mosquitoes.[74]

In a 2009 investigation geared towards determining mosquito dependence on temperature, researcher Kevin D. Lafferty concluded that tropical mosquitoes such as anopheles species (transmit malaria) require temperatures above 16°C to complete their life cycles.[75]

The overall global distribution of malaria is still an area of active research, but nevertheless climate change increases the ideal conditions for the Anopheles mosquito carrying malaria.

Some of us have learned about the Global Malaria Eradication Program in history books, where they detail the time during which malaria was on the verge of worldwide elimination back in the 1950s. In the end, the U.S. and other developed countries successfully eliminated the disease in their own countries, but malaria maintained a major presence in undeveloped and developing nations, and this is still true to this day. Contrary to expectations of historical progress, our generation will grow up to see the retrogression of the spread of malaria: the widening of the scope of malaria, from the tropics to new locations.

Discussing the potential reintroduction of malaria to eradicated zones due to climate change is just painful; history has been there and we certainly do not want to retrograde to that level again.

In Part IV, methods to protect and prevent the predicted spread of malaria will be thoroughly explained.

West Nile Virus

This virus is of the genus *Flavivirus*, which also comprises the Zika virus, yellow fever, and dengue fever. Thus, an understanding of the West Nile Virus would apply to all the aforementioned diseases, amplifying the extent of emerging infectious vector-borne diseases.

As for the details, the West Nile Virus is primarily transmitted by mosquitoes, but hosts can also include birds. Due to the fact that birds can also be hosts, the virus is endemic in a wide range of climates and extends the virus' range of movement across the world. The virus is transmitted during June to September (summer months during dryness) and needs access to an aquatic environment (stagnant or freshwater) to lay eggs.

Published in the journal *Philosophical Transactions of the Royal Society B: Biological Sciences,* a study attempting to determine a clear link between the West Nile Virus and climate change impacts found that recent changes in climatic conditions, particularly increased ambient temperature and fluctuations in rainfall amounts, contributed to the maintenance (endemization process) of WNV in various locations in southern Europe, western Asia, the eastern Mediterranean, the Canadian Prairies, parts of the USA and Australia.[76]

Symptoms

- The majority of cases are asymptomatic (over 70%), leading to an under-reporting of actual cases.

- "20% to 30% [of cases] develop acute systemic febrile illness, which may include headache, myalgias (muscle pains), rash, or gastrointestinal symptoms; fewer than 1% experience neuroinvasive disease." [77]

- An unsettling fact is that many may not know they carry the virus, and there is no known medicinal vaccine.

Climate Change Effect

Warmer temperatures lead to the acceleration of many biological processes of transmission:

- Longer mosquito life cycle.

- Increased contact and rate of mosquito bites between vector (mosquito) and host (bird).

- Hot temperatures are correlated with drought, leading to scarce water distribution. This leads to closer proximity between mosquitoes and birds in swampy regions (trees and stagnant water).

- Higher viral replication rates in mosquitoes, allowing them to pass on the virus to humans in shorter time.

- During drought conditions, standing water pools become richer in the organic material that mosquitoes need in order to thrive. Therefore there is more risk of the West Nile Virus being 'at large' due to ideal conditions for mosquitoes when there is a particular pattern of drought and rainfall. [78]

As explained earlier, the virus is finding new endemic zones and threatening new populations, including Russia, Australia, Greece, U.S., Israel. With no vaccine or medicine, this emerging infectious disease poses a serious threat to a major chunk of the globe, which will be increased by the impacts of climate change.

Nipah Virus (NIP)

You probably haven't heard of this particular virus, which was only discovered in 1999. Its 'reservoir host' is a certain species of fruit bats, but it can be transmitted to people, and then potentially transmitted from person to person via contaminated food, for example.[79]

Symptoms include:

- Fever, drowsiness, penetration of central nervous system within 24 to 48 hours, and coma (potentially leading to death)

- 3 out of 10 people wake up from the coma suffering permanent neurological damage.[79]

The increase in the incidence of this disease has taken place due to the results of human activity, including the impacts of global warming.

As already mentioned, the virus is carried by fruit bats, whose natural habitat is the forests. When this habitat is destroyed due to deforestation and forest fires, the bats migrate into villages. This is how humans are brought into closer contact with the virus.

As explained in an Indian article detailing background information of the Nipah Virus, in Malaysia in 1997-98, the loss of the fruit bats' habitat due to deforestation in addition to a severe drought played an important role in fruit bat migration into the villages.[80] There was also a shortage of food due to forest fires. Due to the drought and resulting fruit bat migration, the incidence of disease linked to the Nipah virus spiked rapidly in 1999.

Because trees absorb carbon dioxide, deforestation in Malaysia and equatorial regions such as the Amazon, Central Africa and Southeast Asia is accountable for 15% of carbon-emissions caused by human activities (reversal of carbon sinks), as documented in a *Telegraph* article discussing the rapid rate of Malaysian defor-estation.[81]

Vector-borne disease is often worsened by climate change, as vectors are attracted to tropical locations. Climate change provides geographic ideals for the spread of tropical disease such as the Nipah Virus. The reduction of global warming's effect means the prevention of these devastating diseases, so let's get working to save human lives!

PART IV

ADAPTATIONS AND SOLUTIONS

The power of human action has the ability to solve major issues and confront challenges in society. Some of the numerous historical examples include racial equality, national independence, and recognition of the importance of the environment. Throughout the 1960s and 70s, for instance, several landmark environmental regulations (i.e. the Clean Air Act and Motor Vehicle Air Pollution Control Act) bolstered awareness of air pollution, derived from excessive emissions of greenhouse gases (greenhouse gas). The Clean Air Act, in particular, was amended several times to ensure the health of the citizens of the United States, and the enforcement of these regulations inspired the world to take heed of the destructive impacts of greenhouse gas on human health.

Moving towards the future, the projected exponential increase in greenhouse gas emissions is bound to proliferate numerous health concerns: not only air pollution, but also heat, and water-borne and vector-borne illness (as covered in Part III). These health concerns must be acted upon. As one of the younger generations who will inherit this Earth, we must administer action towards combating global warming; doing so will make our actions serve as an example for future generations. Hopefully, in the far future, the now-impending issue of global warming will no longer be as great of a threat. Part IV thoroughly explores opportunities for the young generation to solve issues in small, yet meaningful ways.

First and foremost, social media awareness is the very symbol of teenage youth in the 21st century. Let's face it. We all love scrolling through Instagram for fashion and goofing off on Snapchat with filters. However, something even more incredible and impactful would be using these tools as a platform: raising widespread awareness from the mere taps on a screen. If you've made it here, you understand what we face as a society. Others need to understand too, so let's make it count! Post something on your stories and share your concerns! As it is, global warming makes the newspaper headlines on a daily basis, but when it begins to penetrate the very core of the teenage identity — social media — the topic will become a real concern, leading to sparks of sympathy amongst the younger generation. So, let's bring these ideas to billions around the world and be the difference that the planet needs!

Beyond the virtual reality of social media, other solutions can be explored in the realm of politics and congressional legislation. As covered in depth in the *Politicization* chapter of Part I, lobbying is a form of action that can speak volumes about a certain issue. For instance, the horrendous Parkland shooting in February 2018 once again prompted the debate of gun control. Not only was the topic revisited, but students took action and conducted the March for Our Lives on March 24, 2018 in the heart of the nation's capital, Washington D.C. They successfully achieved a Florida state law that raised the minimum age for buying rifles from 18 to 21, and would ramp up on school protection. This effort by Parkland survivors truly embodies the power of human spirit; this same spirit must be targeted toward those congressmen who remain skeptical of climate change. Working together, our voice can augment political pressure for legislative action on climate change. Moreover, some of the readers of this book may be able to vote. I call upon you all to use your right to vote, and your power to share your opinion through the democratic process means. However, it is important to understand that those under 18 can still play a significant role. Organizing rallies and campaigning for climate policies are only a few of the many opportunities that the younger generation can seize. Go explore and make a difference out there!

On a more business-related note, the high emissions of certain companies in the oil and gas sector need to be made accountable for their destructive actions. One way to ensure that these companies have learned their lesson is through the organization of business campaigns. We need these businesses to understand their role in the process, and for them to eventually deliver pledges that will restrict future greenhouse gas emissions and lobbying attempts. These pledges by a business can help serve as a model for future corporations. By avoiding the mistakes of the past, we can diminish businesses' sphere of influence within our very own government.

In addition to the political domain, simple lifestyle changes can effectively ease the number of greenhouse gas released. Take, for instance, our teenage rite of passage: driving a car. Gradually, the driveway becomes packed with cars as the children go through adolescence in a household. Don't get me wrong — this noteworthy tradition in the American household has persisted for decades. However, it would be in the best interest for the younger generations to have a change of preference towards lower-emitting, electric vehicles. The love for the massive, gas-guzzling cars is analogous to a parasitic relationship: while teenagers take pride in their cars, the Earth is negatively affected by the emission of carbon dioxide gas.

Another convenient solution is carpooling. Reducing the amount of cars on the road with an increasing population and saving gas by riding with others is an excellent option. Additionally, Elon Musk's project "The Boring Company" aspires to build a hyperloop throughout an elaborate underground system in Los Angeles. This example of public transportation should be chosen over the exorbitant use of cars, which would save millions of tons of carbon dioxide gas from the transportation sector (comprising 14% of total U.S. emissions). So, little by little, let's sprinkle in those changes in regards to how we transport ourselves, and do so in a manner that minimizes greenhouse gas emissions!

Above all else, implications on human health are the most drastic. The full scope of consequences were explored in Part III so here, we will just briefly recall some of the health impacts and some simple solutions that can be practiced.

This first solution scares the majority of the youth today: reading. Becoming informed is of utmost importance as destructive climatic effects are more frequent. Keep up on the daily headlines, find out what is going on around the world, and how it may affect your specific community. For instance, this entire book investigates climatic and health effects of global warming on both worldwide and nationwide levels. Apply this information to your own community, and recent abnormalities in the weather. For instance, I live in Orange County in Southern California. The mere thought of wildfires invoke caution and warning, but nonetheless I am fully aware that a fire can incite anytime, anywhere. Specifically, be aware of the "burn zone" (aka literally all of California). The omnipresent threats of wildfires should therefore inspire any at-risk resident to minimize the possibility of a wildfire to spark. One solution that I myself practice is getting rid of dry vegetation near my home. In the terrible (but plausible) case that a fire sparks near my home, getting rid of any dry plants that may serve as "food" for the expanding fire could be extremely important.

Additionally, on the note of wildfires, the worsening of air quality is truly a deep issue for communities affected by wildfires. This implication in human health is very apparent — currently, 7 million people die from health-damaging air pollution each year. This combination of fine particulate matter and ozone pollution is clearly devastating and by the looks of it, the death rates are expected to rise. However, that doesn't mean that *we* cannot adapt. In fact, adaptation is what humans do best. For instance, P100 masks and N95 respirators need to be accessible at a widespread level for people to live with poor air quality. Specifically, chronic obstructive pulmonary disease (COPD) is one chronic illness that may play a key role in the devastating figure above. So let's ensure that we are mindful of air quality everyday, and prepare to adaptations as we grow older. It doesn't sound like much fun, but we must prepare convenient, ingenious solutions to be able to facilitate the one process that keeps us alive: breathing.

Another implication on health is foodborne/waterborne illness. Caused by excessive flooding, the rampant impact on health can be attributed to pathogenic organisms. One common solution is to steer clear of dirty water, and to ensure that all food is healthy and properly managed. As we grow up, edible food and drinking water may be compromised due to serious climatic effects (i.e. frequent flooding). So let us ensure we only consume healthy food, and adopt clean practices to maintain health.

The final health implication relates to mosquito-borne illness. According to the 2018 National Climate Assessment, the expansion of mosquito-borne illnesses, including malaria, West Nile virus, and dengue fever, is projected to spread across a wide geographic area (covered in Part III). As daunting as this seems, preventive measures can be taken through vaccinations and treatments such as antimalarials, mosquito nets. Nevertheless, the emerging infectious diseases are only beginning to be transmitted, developing serious fears of vector-borne disease. So at this time, the younger generation must brace themselves for any situation. Be wary of signs of any mosquito-borne illness near you, and ensure that repellent is always nearby in case of emergency. Moreover, mosquitoes tend to breed over stagnant pools of water; eliminating these puddles in your community could be crucial to reducing the possibility of a mosquito breeding site.

Overall, my passion comes from learning about global warming and its especially devastating impacts on human health. My passion for the healthcare industry was spurred from an early age; both of my parents being doctors, I was lucky to be exposed to science at such a young age. Coupled with this was the serious implications of global warming on human health, and having visited a travel clinic, I have learned of the severe health challenges in developing countries where mosquito-borne, water-borne, and foodborne illness is prevalent.

Reflecting on my journey as I have written this book, I have learned numerous invaluable lessons about not only the content, but also how to channel my focus and pour my heart into a work. I have learned perseverance through it all, and the power of words as an effective medium to communicate with others. I have understood the revelation that I am only sixteen years old, but have the blessed opportunity to share my knowledge with others in my generation in hopes of changing society for the better in the future. Thank you, and let's raise awareness and defeat global warming!

FOOTNOTES

Part I

1. Stocker, T.F., et al. (2013). Climate Change 2013: The Physical Science Basis. *Fifth Assessment Report of the Intergovernmental Panel on Climate Change.* Cambridge, UK and New York, NY: Cambridge University Press.

2. Mandeville, Charles. (2018, January 18). *USGS: Volcano Hazards Program CVO Mount Hood,* U.S. Geographical Survey. Reston, VA: U.S. Geographical Survey.

3. Lallanila, Marc. "What Is the Greenhouse Effect?", *Live-Science,* www.livescience.com/37743-greenhouse-effect. html, (7 March 2018).

4. "Greenhouse Gases: Water Vapor", National Oceanic and Atmospheric Administration, www.ncdc.noaa.gov/monitoring-references/faq/greenhouse-gases.php?section=watervapor, (2018).

5. Naik, Gautam. "Slowdown in Warming Tied to Less Water Vapor", *The Wall Street Journal,* www.wsj.com/articles/SB10001424052748704194504575031404275769886, (29 Jan. 2010).

6. Raupach, M. R., et al. (2013). "The Declining Uptake Rate of Atmospheric CO_2 by Land and Ocean Sinks." Vol. 10, No. 11. Canberra, Australia: Biogeosciences, 18407–18454.

7. Understanding Global Warming Potentials," Environmental Protection Agency, www.epa.gov/ghgemissions/

understanding-global-warming-potentials, (February 14, 2017).

8. National Research Council (2010). *Advancing the Science of Climate Change*. Washington, DC: The National Academies Press.

9. S. Solomon, et al. (2007). *Climate Change 2007: The Physical Science Basis. Fourth Assessment Report of the Intergovernmental Panel on Climate Change*. Cambridge, UK: Cambridge University Press.

10. The Editors of Encyclopedia Britannica, "Nitrogen Cycle," www.britannica.com/science/nitrogen-cycle, (March 15, 2018).

11. O. Edenhofer, et al. Climate Change 2014: Mitigation of Climate Change. *Fifth Assessment Report of the Intergovernmental Panel on Climate Change*. Cambridge, UK and New York, NY: Cambridge University Press.

12. Steinfeld, Henning, et al. (1 January 2006). *Livestock's Long Shadow: Environmental Issues and Options*. Rome, Italy: Food and Agriculture Organization.

13. Sanders, Robert. "Fertilizer Use Responsible for Increase in Nitrous Oxide in Atmosphere." *Berkeley News*, news.berkeley.edu/2012/04/02/fertilizer-use-responsible-for-increase-in-nitrous-oxide-in-atmosphere.com, (July 2015).

14. "China Statistical Yearbook," National Bureau of Statistics of China, www.stats.gov.cn/tjsj/ndsj/2017/indexeh.html, (2017).

15. Zhiqiang, Zhang. (2017) "Climate Change Science Dynamic Monitoring Express, 2017, Issue 9." Lanzhou, China: Chinese Academy of Sciences.

16. Huang, Jinxia, et al. (31 May 2010). *Climate Change and China's Agricultural Sector: An Overview of Impacts, Adaptation and Mitigation.* Geneva, Switzerland: International Centre for Trade and Sustainable Development. vii-viii.

17. "Inventory of U.S. Greenhouse Gas Emissions and Sinks 1990-2018," EPA, https://www.epa.gov/ghgemissions/inventory-us-greenhouse-gas-emissions-and-sinks, (2018).

18. "Electricity Explained - Basics," U.S. Energy Information Administration, https://www.eia.gov/tools/faqs/faq.php?id=427&t=3, (2016).

19. "Summary of GHG Emissions for Russian Federation," United Nations Climate Change Secretariat, unfccc.int/files/ghg_emissions_data/application/pdf/rus_ghg_profile, (2012).

20. Bhawan, Indira P. (December 2015). *India: First Biennial Update Report to the United Nations Framework Convention on Climate Change.* New Delhi, India: Ministry of Environment, Forest and Climate Change.

21. The Editors of Encyclopaedia Britannica, "Lobbying", Encyclopædia Britannica, Inc., www.britannica.com/topic/lobbying, (14 Sept. 2017).

22. *Corporate Carbon Policy Footprint.* (2017). London, UK: InfluenceMap.

23. "Lobbying Spending Database Oil & Gas, 2018." *OpenSecrets*, Center for Responsive Politics, www.opensecrets.org/lobby/indusclient.php?id=E01&year=2018, (24 July 2018).

24. Delmas, Magali, et al. (2016). "Corporate Environmental Performance and Lobbying." Vol. 2, No. 2, Los Angeles, CA: Academy of Management Discoveries, 175–197.

Part II

25. Dunne, John P., et al. (2013). "Reductions in Labour Capacity from Heat Stress under Climate Warming." Vol. 3, No. 6. Princeton, New Jersey: Nature Climate Change, 563–566.

26. National Research Council (2011). *Climate Stabilization Targets: Emissions, Concentrations, and Impacts over Decades to Millennia.*. Washington, DC: The National Academies Press.

27. Kench, Paul, et al. (February 2018). "Patterns of Island Change and Persistence Offer Alternate Adaptation Pathways for Atoll Nations." Published online by *Nature Communications*. Vol. 9, No. 1.

28. Friedman, Thomas L. "Can Egypt Pull Together?," *New York Times*, https://www.nytimes.com/2013/07/07/opinion/sunday/friedman-can-egypt-pull-together.html, (7 July 2013).

29. Caldeira, K., and M. E. Wickett. (2003). *Oceanography: Anthropogenic Carbon and Ocean pH*. Livermore, CA: Nature, 425, 365.

30. Orr, J. C. et al. (2005). *Anthropogenic Ocean Acidification over the Twenty-first Century and its Impact on Calcifying Organisms*. Princeton, New Jersey: Nature, 437, 681-686.

31. Walsh, J., et al. (2014). *Ch. 2: Our Changing Climate. Climate Change Impacts in the United States: The Third National Climate Assessment*. J. M. Melillo, Terese (T.C.) Richmond, and G. W. Yohe, Eds., Washington, DC: U.S. Government Printing Office, 19-67.

32. Clarkson, M. O., et al. (September 2015). "Ocean Acidification and the Permian-Triassic Mass Extinction." Vol. 348, No. 6231. Edinburgh, UK: *Science*, 229–232.

33. Kharin, V. V., et al. (2013). *Changes in Temperature and Precipitation Extremes in the CMIP5 Ensemble.* Victoria, Canada: *Climatic Change*, 119, 345-357.

34. Cayan, D. R., et al. (2010) *Future Dryness in the Southwest US and the Hydrology of the Early 21st Century Drought.* Danvers, MA: National Academy of Sciences, 107, 21271-21276.

35. Westerling, A. L., et al. (2011). "Continued Warming Could Transform Greater Yellowstone Fire Regimes by mid-21st Century." Published online by *Proceedings of the National Academy of Sciences of the United States of America*, 108, 13165-13170.

36. Fleshler, David. "The World Has Never Seen a Category 6 Hurricane. But the Day May Be Coming", *Los Angeles Times*, https://www.latimes.com/nation/la-na-hurricane-strenth-20180707-story.html, (7 July 2018).

37. Gutmann, Ethan D., et al. (May 2018). "Changes in Hurricanes from a 13-Yr Convection-Permitting Pseudo-Global Warming Simulation." Published online by *Journal of Climate*.

Part III

38. Deschênes, Olivier, and Michael Greenstone. (October 2011). "Climate Change, Mortality, and Adaptation: Evidence from Annual Fluctuations in Weather in the US." Published online by *American Economic Journal: Applied Economics*.

39. "Heat Stroke: Symptoms and Treatment", WebMD, www.webmd.com/a-to-z-guides/heat-stroke-symptoms-and-treatment#1, (2018).

40. Axelrod YK, Diringer MN (May 2008). "Temperature Management in Acute Neurologic Disorders." Published online by *Neurol. Clin,* 585–603, xi.

41. Anderson, G. B., et al. (2013). "Heat-related Emergency Hospitalizations for Respiratory Diseases in the Medicare Population." Published online by *American Journal of Respiratory and Critical Care Medicine,* 187, 1098-1103.

42. Baaghideh, Mohammad, et al. (2017). "Climate Change and Simulation of Cardiovascular Disease Mortality: A Case Study of Mashhad, Iran." Mashbad, Iran: *Iranian Journal of Public Health,* 396–407.

43. Fletcher, B. A., et al. (2012). "Association of Summer Temperatures with Hospital Admissions for Renal Diseases in New York State: A Case-Crossover Study." Published online by *American Journal of Epidemiology,* 175, 907-916.

44. Fakheri, R. J., and D. S. Goldfarb (2011). "Ambient Temperature as a Contributor to Kidney Stone Formation: Implications of Global Warming." Published online by *Kidney International,* 79, 1178-1185.

45. Kim Knowlton, et al. (November 1, 2007). "Projecting Heat-Related Mortality Impacts Under a Changing Climate in the New York City Region." Published online by *American Journal of Public Health.* Vol 97, No. 1, 2028-2034.

46. Lin, S., et al. (2012). "Excessive Heat and Respiratory Hospitalizations in New York State: Estimating Current and Future Public Health Burden Related to Climate Change." Published online by *Environmental Health Perspectives,* 120, 1571-1577.

47. Fowler, D, Amann, et al. "Ground-Level Ozone in the 21st Century: Future Trends, Impacts and Policy Implications." London, UK: Royal Society Science Policy.

48. "Ground-Level Ozone Basics." Digital Image. Environmental Protection Agency. October 31, 2018. Accessed December 2, 2018. www.epa.gov/ground-level-ozone-pollution/ground-level-ozone-basics#effects.

49. "Climate Change Impacts on the United States: The Potential Consequences of Climate Variability and Change." Digital Image. GlobalChange. 2001. Accessed October 27, 2018. www.usgcrp.gov/usgcrp/Library/nationalassessment/00Intro.pdf.

50. Jacob, D.J., et al. (2009). "Effect of Climate Change on Air Quality." Published online by *Atmospheric Environment.* 51–63.

51. Fann, et al. (2015) "The Geographic Distribution and Economic Value of Climate Change-related Ozone health Impacts in the United States in 2030." Published online by *Journal of the Air & Waste Management Association,* 65, 570-580.

52. "Health Effects of Ozone Pollution," Environmental Protection Agency, www.epa.gov/ozone-pollution/health-effects-ozone-pollution, (27 Feb. 2017).

53. "Health Effects of Ozone Pollution," Sleep Aider Community, www.sleepaider.com/articles/health-effects-of-ozone-pollution.22/, (20 Oct. 2017).

54. Perera, Elizabeth Martin, and Todd Sanford. "Rising Temperatures, Worsening Ozone Pollution," *Union of Concerned Scientists USA,* www.ucsusa.org/sites/default/files/legacy/assets/documents/global_warming/climate-change-and-ozone-pollution.pdf, (June 2011).

55. Jerrett, M., et al. (2009). "Long-term Ozone Exposure and Mortality." Published online by *New England Journal of Medicine*, 360, 1085-1095.

56. Spracklen, D. V., et al. (2009). "Impacts of Climate Change from 2000 to 2050 on Wildfire Activity and Carbonaceous Aerosol Concentrations in the western United States." Published online by *Journal of Geophysical Research: Atmospheres*, 114.

57. Environmental Protection Agency, (2009). *Integrated Science Assessment for Particulate Matter*. Research Triangle Park, NC: National Center for Environmental Assessment.

58. "Asthma," National Heart Lung and Blood Institute, U.S. Department of Health and Human Services, www.nhlbi. nih.gov/health-topics/asthma, n.d.

59. Bloom, B., et al. (2013). *Summary Health Statistics for U.S. Children: National Health Interview Survey, 2012*. Hyattsville, MD: National Center for Health Statistics.

60. Kraker, Dan. "Researchers Search for Clues to Toxic Algae Blooms." Digital Image. Minnesota Public Radio News. August 7, 2017. Accessed December 5, 2018. www.mprnews.org/story/2017/08/17/researchers-search-for-clues-to-toxic-algae-blooms.

61. Environmental Protection Agency. (2004). "Report to Congress: Impacts and Control of CSOs and SSOs." Washington, DC: Office of Water.

62. Messner, M., et al. (2006). "An Approach for Developing a National Estimate of Waterborne Disease due to Drinking Water and a National Estimate Model Application." Published online by *Journal of Water and Health*, 201-240.

63. Hribar, C. (2010). "Understanding Concentrated Animal Feeding Operations and Their Impact on Communities." Bowling Green, OH: National Association of Local Boards of Health, 22.

64. Drayna, P., et al. (24 May 2010). "Association Between Rainfall and Pediatric Emergency Department Visits for Acute Gastrointestinal Illness." Milwaukee, WI: *Environmental Health Perspectives*, 118, 1439-1443.

65. Patz, J. A., et al. (2008). "Climate Change and Waterborne Disease Risk in the Great Lakes Region of the U.S." Published online by *American Journal of Preventive Medicine*, 35, 451-458.

66. Vereen, E., et al. (2013). "Landscape and Seasonal Factors Influence *Salmonella* and *Campylobacter* Prevalence in a Rural Mixed Use Watershed." Published online by *Water Research*, 47, 6075-6085.

67. Gingold, D. B., et al. (2014). "Ciguatera Fish Poisoning and Climate Change: Analysis of National Poison Center Data in the United States, 2001–2011." Published online by *Environmental Health Perspectives*, 122, 580-586.

68. Xu, Z., et al. (2012). "Climate Change and Children's Health—A Call for Research on What Works to Protect Children." Published online by *International Journal of Environmental Research and Public Health*, 9, 3298-3316.

69. Dechet, A. M., et al. (2008). "Non-foodborne Vibrio Infections: An Important Cause of Morbidity and Mortality in the United States, 1997–2006." Published online by *Clinical Infectious Diseases*, 46, 970-976.

70. "Malaria: Overview and Symptoms", *MayoClinic*, https://www.mayoclinic.org/diseases-conditions/malaria/symptoms-causes/syc-20351184, (December 2018).

71. Cyril Caminade, et al. (2014). "Impact of Climate Change on Global Malaria Distribution." Published online by *Proceedings of the National Academy of Sciences*, 111, 3286-3291.

72. Arab A, et al. (2014). "Modelling the Effects of Weather and Climate on Malaria Distributions in West Africa." Published online by *Malaria Journal.* 13, 126.

73. Ahlenius, Hugo. "Climate Change and Malaria." Digital Image. GRID-Arendal. February 21, 2012. Accessed November 6, 2018. http://old.grida.no/graphicslib/detail/climate-change-and-malaria-scenario-for-2050_bffe#

74. Chaves LF, et al. (2012). "Indian Ocean Dipole and Rainfall Drive a Moran Effect in East Africa Malaria Transmission." Published online by *J Infect Dis.* 205, 1885–1891.

75. Lafferty, Kevin D. (1 April 2009). "The Ecology of Climate Change and Infectious Diseases." Published online by *Ecological Society of America,* 90, 888-900.

76. Paz, S. (5 April 2015). "Climate Change Impacts on West Nile Virus Transmission in a Global Context." University of Haifa, Israel: Department of Geography and Environmental Studies. Vol. 370, No. 1665.

77. Petersen, L. R., et al. (2013). "Estimated Cumulative Incidence of West Nile Virus Infection in US Adults, 1999-2010." Published online by *Epidemiology & Infection*, 141, 591-595.

78. Eisen, W. K., et al. (2008) "Impact of Climate Variation on Mosquito Abundance in California." Published online by *Journal of Vector Ecology*, 33, 89-98.

79. Davis, Charles P. "Nipah Virus Infection", *MedicineNet*, https://www.medicinenet.com/nipah_virus_infection/article.htm#nipah_virus_infection_niv_facts, (May 2018).

80. Chakravarty, Ambar, et al. (2006). "Nipah Virus Encephalitis: A Cause for Concern for Indian Neurologists?" Kolkata, India: Annals of Indian Academy of Neurology. Vol. 9, No. 3, 137.

81. "Malaysia Destroying its Forests Three Times Faster than all Asia Combined," *The Telegraph*, https://www.telegraph.co.uk/news/earth, (February 2011).

APPENDIX 1

TERMS

Part I

Chapter 1:

- **Sinusoidal** — This word describes the up-and-down nature of a continuous sine wave; a peak transforms into a trough and this repeats itself.

- **Fossil Fuels** — These natural fuels are derived from sources such as coal and gas.

- **Greenhouse Gases** — These gases absorb infrared radiation from the sun, and ultimately contribute to the warming of the Earth.

Chapter 2:

- **Global Warming** — The central topic of this book, global warming is the long-term rise in Earth's average temperature.

- **Climate Change** — This term refers to a change in the climate/weather that may last for long periods of time; it can be seen as the result of global warming and increase in atmospheric greenhouse gas concentration.

- **Solar Radiation** — This phrase simply refers to any energy derived from the sun.

- **Greenhouse Effect** — This process details how solar energy is trapped in the lower atmosphere, leading to the eventual warming of the Earth.

- **Global Warming Potential (GWP)** — As a form of measurement, GWP analyzes exactly how much a specific greenhouse gas would warm Earth's atmosphere.

- **Positive Feedback Loop** — This cycle explains that after an initial warming, a specific phenomenon would further increase that warming (e.g. water vapor as a greenhouse gas).

- **Absolute Humidity** — This term describes the ability of the air to hold water vapor, and can be shortened to its more conventional form: humidity.

- **Land and Ocean Sinks** — These are locations which absorb gases (mainly carbon dioxide) from Earth's atmosphere.

- **Nitrogen Cycle** — This biological process can be explained by the interconversion of nitrogen compounds in both the environment and living organisms (e.g. nitrogen fixation).

- **Anthropogenic** — This term refers to anything that is human-caused.

- **Enteric Fermentation** — This digestive process refers to how carbohydrates are broken down into simple molecules for absorption; cows practice this form of digestion, leading to the release of methane.

- **Aerobic Decomposition** — This process refers to the breakdown of organic molecules in the presence of oxygen.

- **Methanogens** — These are microorganisms that produce methane when there is little amounts of oxygen present.

Chapter 3:

- **Lobbying** — This term refers to the action of attempting to influence a person (usually a politician) about an issue through various means.

Part II

Chapter 4:

- **Rising Temperatures** — This term is the observable rise in average Earth surface temperature and the primary indication of the existence of global warming.

Chapter 5:

- **Sea Level Rise** — This phenomenon refers to the observable rise in sea level across the Earth's oceans; the melting of ice sheets and glaciers cause the ice to transform into liquid water.

- **Thermal Expansion** — This term describes how matter can change shape, area, and volume in response to temperature; in our case, sea water may expand due to increased sea temperatures.

- **Gulf Stream** — This term refers to a warm Atlantic ocean current originating in the Gulf of Mexico, stretching to Florida, and moving up the eastern seaboard.

- **Representative Pathway Concentrations** — This term is used by the reports of the Intergovernmental Panel on Climate Change (IPCC) to predict possible trajectories of greenhouse gas emissions in the future, and what the effects of each scenario are (for e.g., RCP2.5 would mean lower greenhouse gas concentration and thus less sea level rise when compared to RCP8.5).

Chapter 6:

- **Ocean Acidification** — The process listed here refers to the eventual acidification of the ocean due to an increased concentration of H^+ ions, thus lowering the pH.

- **Acidity** — This chemical concept is directly linked to H^+ ions; more hydrogen ions in a liquid medium results in higher acidity levels.

- **pH** — Also accompanied with acidity is pH. This numerical scale from 1-14 identifies how acidic or basic a given substance is: 1 being the most acidic, 7 being neutral, and 14 being the most basic.

- **Permian-Triassic Mass Extinction** — An extinction event about 252 million years ago in which ocean acidification played a role due to high atmospheric carbon dioxide concentration.

- **Ocean Stratification** — This phenomenon occurs when water with different density or temperature forms layers.

Chapter 7:

- **Extreme Events** — These refer to the rare and extreme phenomena (i.e. wildfires, hurricanes, flooding, heat waves); global warming is expected to increase the likelihood of these.

Part III

Chapter 8:

- **Heat Stroke** — This health condition refers to when the core body temperature exceeds 104 degrees Fahrenheit, leading to problems in the central nervous system.

- **Hyperthermia** — This health condition simply refers to the case in which a human body temperature is greatly above normal.

- **Chronic Disease** — This type of disease (the other being infectious disease) must last at least 3 months; it gradually progresses in the human body and cannot necessarily be prevented by vaccine or disappear.

- **Kidney Stones** — These are hard deposits made of minerals and salts that may form in one's kidneys.

- **Urban Heat Island** — This term refers to a metropolitan area that may be much warmer than rural areas nearby because of human activity (e.g. New York City compared to rural New York).

Chapter 9:

- **Ground-level Ozone** — The chemical compound O_3 can be very damaging when in the troposphere zone, causing damage to humans and other organisms.

- **Volatile Organic Compounds (VOCs)** — These are compounds that easily become gases; they are released from the burning of fossil fuels.

- **Air Quality Index** — This numerical system is a way to measure the air quality, with categories ranging from healthy to extremely hazardous air.

- **Particulate Matter (PM)** — These are microscopic solid or liquid matter suspended in the atmosphere of Earth; one subcategory is fine particulate matter, in which the diameter of the particulates are less than 2.5 microns.

- **Asthma** — This respiratory condition refers to when a person's airways are one of the following: inflamed, narrow, swell up, or produce too much mucus; this makes may cause breathing difficulty.

Chapter 10:

- **Algal Blooms** — These regions in water refer to the rapid increase or accumulation in the population of algae, and can be very harmful with lower oxygen levels.

Chapter 11:

- **Vectors** — These organisms transmit a disease or parasite from one animal or plant to another (i.e. mosquitoes).

Made in the USA
Middletown, DE
26 March 2019